# DIARY of a mad GAY MAN

# DIARY *of a* mad GAY MAN

## JEREMY TAYLOR

NEW YORK QUEER PUBLISHING
NEW YORK

Copyright © 2020 by Jeremy Taylor
All rights reserved. Names, characters, places, and incidents may be the product of the author's imagination or are used fictitiously or have been changed, and any resemblance to actual persons, living or dead, businesses, companies, events, or locales is entirely coincidental.

New York Queer Publishing
1420 York Avenue
New York, NY 10021

No parts of this book may be reproduced, scanned, or distributed in any printed or electronic form without permission. Please do not participate in or encourage piracy of copyrighted materials in violation of the author's rights.

Taylor, Jeremy // Diary of a Mad Gay Man
Jeremy, Taylor // New York Queer Publishing

Library of Congress Control Number: 2020917494
ISBN 9781735257433

Purchase only authorized editions.

I dedicate this book to Joan Rivers.
Gone too soon.

*I don't exercise. If God had wanted me to bend over, he would have put diamonds on the floor.*

–JOAN RIVERS

*... people are hung sometimes ...*

−JOAN OF ARC

*... and sometimes they are not ...*

—JEREMY TAYLOR

# SENTIMENTAL NOTE

Ten years ago, my life was rough. I had recently immigrated to the United States from Russia and planned never to return to avoid getting prosecuted for being gay. Receiving the status of political asylee had been a strenuous process, and getting "Asylum Granted" stamped was like winning the lottery. No, ma'am, I was never going back.

At that time, I had a job as a personal assistant—"Do this," "Do that," that kind of thing—and was making ten dollars an hour, but it was five dollars an hour that I was living on. The other half was being withheld by my boss to pay him back the ten grand he'd lent me for my asylum lawyer.

At the time, I was twenty-something—I am not trying to be vague; I barely remember what happened five seconds ago, let alone in my twenties—and I was living in a basement apartment with four roommates. To survive (even if my rent was somewhat low) I shared my bed—you read that right, my bed—with a straight female stripper, which brought me an extra two hundred a month.

I stayed optimistic by reading and writing comedy, but my life was anything but funny. People choose fiction because fiction helps us escape reality, and reading was essential to me. My boss was incredibly demanding, but I couldn't quit because I owed him money. In the meantime a friend of mine gave me a

DVD of Joan Rivers. The DVD was a documentary called *A Piece of Work*. My friend knew I loved comedy, and he thought I would like it.

I did not like it.

I fucking *loved* it!

In the documentary, Joan Rivers talks about how hard it was to find a job at her age, and it clicked with me that life was similar for an immigrant.

Joan had to reinvent herself so she wrote a book. Her book—*I Hate Everyone, Starting with Me*—was hysterical, the kind of comedy I love reading. If that book were pasta puttanesca,[1] I would stuff it in my mouth daily.

Once, while reading my new book on the subway, I cried from laughter. Joan Rivers had become my inspiration, so it was time to reinvent myself the way she had.

As soon as I paid off the loan to my boss, I quit and moved to Denver. Quitting and letting go was the most liberating experience, but—and it is a colossal *but*—two years later, I returned to the same job because I missed New York.

You're wondering: Was I stupid?

Yes.

No.

Maybe.

I was offered a sum of money I couldn't refuse, and the job was fine until late 2018.

Three things were happening then: I was at a job I hated because I was stagnating, I had recently graduated from culinary school but hated working at a restaurant—which was twenty-one grand worth of a wasted degree—and, somehow, I had gotten into a huge credit card debt.

I felt like I was back where I started. I felt stuck and adrift at sea, my mental health stagnating.

Then—yes, there is a *then*—I remembered my best friend: Joan Rivers (may she rest in peace). I immediately ordered her book—*Diary of a Mad Diva*—from Amazon and settled down to read it. The book was hysterical and one of a kind, and after finishing it for the third time, I realized that I either fall down the rabbit hole or reinvent myself.

So I wrote *Diary of a Mad Gay Man*.

This diary is a parody of gay life and pop culture, and if you take anything seriously, see the final note at the end and send your suggestions to Mississippi. I did what I know best: make fun of myself by exaggerating my life and by being shady. But following the advice of my lawyer, Nikita, I changed everyone's name—just in case you bitches wanna come after my money.

Listen, comedy saved my life numerous times whether I was doing standup or publishing funny novels. But remember: if there is no real pain, there is no comedy. This shady diary was made possible by a crisis. My life depended on that change.

One: I was at the same job for the past seven years (a total of ten) going nowhere. Two: I was tired of hooking up and craved companionship. And three: I wanted to save money.

What happened in 2019 is between you and me, OK, bitch?

[1] Puttanesca means whore, by the way, if you were wondering.

# DIARY *of a* mad GAY MAN

# JANUARY

Grindr Bio: Hi, guys, my name is Jeremy. I live in Astoria. I'm 31, 5'8", 140 pounds. Looking for dates! HMU!

## JANUARY 1

*Dear Diary:*

I'm hungover since yesterday I was trashed out of my tight ass. I woke up with wood and a strange desire for a mimosa, so I took care of both straight in the kitchen.

Last year (note: yesterday), I attended a themed New Year's Eve party where we had to dress up as our favorite animals. My favorite cowhide sweater was at the dry cleaners so I showed up as "doggy style."

My costume is hard to describe so let's just say I wore a tail and I'll let you fill in the blanks . . .

Quite frankly animals annoy me because they're smelly, needy, and privileged. Like, when was the last time a cat fed a human for a change?

At the party, my best friend Bagwis asked me to write down three resolutions for the upcoming year, and since there was no paper I wrote them down on toilet paper in the bathroom while giving a hand job. Bagwis said I should write down my resolutions while inebriated to stay true to myself. Sober, Bagwis noted, we can be in denial about our feelings, and we sabotage ourselves from time to time because we don't feel deserving. Bagwis can be a real Oprah sometimes. His advice helps when I need it, but—ugh—it's annoying when I don't!

Since my handwriting sucks (like Daddy, like handwriting) I'm not sure what I wrote, but I deciphered the following:

**1. Exercise more and find a new job.**

To start right away on my goals, I moved some weights and then moved some bowels. I'm an overachiever (said he humbly) and I like accomplishing goals twice. Finding a new job, however, is not something I could fix while sitting on the toilet bowl.

**2. Go on a diet and lose weight.**

This one was easy. I googled a picture of Mama June and I may never eat again. I'm definitely not smoking any meth. Why does anyone think it's appropriate to insert a white fence in your mouth from Home Depot and call it teeth? She doesn't need toothpaste; she needs Murphy's Oil to polish her veneers.

**3. Get a dildo or a boyfriend.**

That's when it struck me that one crucial piece was missing from my life: a boyfriend. I want a deep connection with someone and a constant dick wouldn't hurt either. And why *would* it hurt? Is it eleven inches?

I am single.

I looked at the toilet paper closer, hoping that I'd drunkenly written something else. There was no mistake. Any way you dissect the word "boyfriend" it means you want one.

Unless you dissect like Jack the Ripper, then what you want is an execution.


**JANUARY 2**

*Dear Diary:*

Another resolution of mine is to become less jealous and bitter this year. I'm single, and since most of my friends are in relationships I always feel like the third wheel, especially if it's a threesome. I'm thirty-one (which is the age of Uranus), semi-cute (seventy percent *semi*, and thirty percent *cute*), and live alone and miserable (like a hoarder, but without any cats).

Why am I single? It's not like I have a tail, two assholes, or look like the Elephant Man. I dress well (from H&M), give ten percent of my salary to charity (drag queen performers), and exercise regularly (exercise my right to hook up, that is).

I blame the gay community with its high standards and ageism. Everyone wants a rich, young, skinny bitch—so basically my boss. The other day, I was chatting with a handsome Broadway actor (note: server), but after I sent him my pictures on Grindr he blocked me. I blame my pudgy face.

I learned my face was pudgy while watching ancient porn videos of me on Myspace. To feel better, I remembered that the camera adds ten pounds, or in Angelina Jolie's case, ten children.

"Oh, wow," I told a hookup who came over, "I resemble a whale in that pose!"

The hookup finished his martini and said, "Wait, why are we watching this dumb documentary about whales, bitch? Turn off the Discovery Channel and turn around—"

That night, after my hookup left I googled: *How to not die alone and miserable?*

A plastic surgery website came up.

I made an appointment with a plastic surgeon for the next day.

## JANUARY 3

*Dear Diary:*

My consultation with the plastic surgeon went fabulously well! I haven't been this happy since the price of Imodium went down at my local pharmacy. I'm skipping like a little girl on the corner of Park Avenue and You'll-Soon-Be-Skinny Street.

The surgeon—Dr. Michael Swango—offered a solution to make me skinny by removing buccal fat from my cheeks, which are two tennis ball-shaped globes in my face. No wonder I look like a fucking squirrel! Even though the results would take four months to show up, afterwards my cheeks would be defined and chiseled. We scheduled the surgery for Friday, January 18th.

The only problem standing between the surgery and me becoming a skinny bitch is the six-thousand-dollar price tag. Listen, such an expense means nothing when your vanity's at stake, especially when you've been a cow and a "calf" your entire life. Sarah Palin would know: she is a stupid and a Bristol.

By the way, have you seen Bristol Palin's reality show *Life's a Tripp*? In the pilot, when some fellow tells Bristol, "Your mother's a whore," (which, you know, is true), Bristol insults him, "Are you a homosexual?"

Yes, he was, bitch, and you know how I know? He looked fabulous!

If I were him, I'd say, "Being gay is not something I chose, asshole. And you can't use it against me as if there's something wrong with me. But if I weren't a homosexual, I would *wish* to become one."

But calling him a homosexual is like calling Bristol Palin a ratchet cunt: so obvious.

## JANUARY 4

*Dear Diary:*

No wonder I'm seventy-five thousand dollars in debt! Not only because I'm adding six more thousand for the buccal-fat-removal surgery, but because I live alone in a two-bedroom apartment and should have a roommate to help me split the bills.

That said, I love living alone. I'm a neat-freak for one, and everyone I've lived with to date has behaved like a pig. Plus, you can hear your roommates have sex in the next room through the thin New York walls. I would know. I listened to my straight roommates have sex throughout the past decade and it was boring. If you're fucking, fuck louder!

When I was desperate for cash, I'd rented out the second bedroom for some mad money, but I'm not that desperate.

Yet.

My other expenses include Imodium, laxatives, and poppers—another thousand dollars a month—and of course there's still the matter of the twenty-one thousand in culinary school debt.

Credit card minimum payments barely cover the interest and I wish I could disclose the number of credit cards I own. Let's just say the number is like the age of Bagwis (who's Asian): anywhere between twenty and fifty—you'll never guess. And just today, I opened another credit card to pay for the buccal-fat-removal surgery.

Am I a psycho?

My chiropractor A-wut said, and I quote, "No, I'm not."

I said, "I know *you're* not a psycho. I'm asking if *I* am."

A-wut put an icepack on my shoulder and said, "Obviously, bitch! And not just a psycho but also delusional. Borrowing is no way to live. Sucking dick and getting paid for it is the right way to live. Get yourself a sugar daddy! Bye, see you next week."

In my defense, it's not like I spent a lot of that money on between twenty and fifty knives.

Even if I did (which I might), at least I can explain them by saying I graduated from culinary school, regardless of if it sounds like I graduated from John Wayne Macy's school.

At least my story is more believable than Roseanne Barr blaming Ambien about her Twitter attack on Valerie Jarrett. Roseanne had a show on ABC and she was still too lazy to scroll down to the letter R in her alphabet world and learn something about racism. I'm actually on the letter C and discovered a new word: cunt. Which is how Roseanne Barr's name showed up.

Straight women hate the word "cunt," but drag queens and gay men love it. I love drag queens, and especially the fiercest one: Queen Elizabeth. She and I are real close, and we're even on a first-name basis. I call her Liz.

By the way, Liz says "cunt" all the time, I swear!

I heard the following true scuttlebutt from my friend Daphne Elizabeth III IV X, who lives in London. The other day, Meghan Markel tried to sneak into Liz's bedroom to check out the jewelry collection and screenshot Liz's internet browsing history. Liz caught her and yelled, "You *cunt* go there!" That's what Meghan heard and went in!

But then the guards kicked her out, and that's a whole other issue.

Anyway, I refuse to blame myself for my money issues. I was born in Soviet Russia in 1987 and nobody taught me how to save. We grew up in extreme poverty with a single working mother trying to provide for two children, one of whom (not me) ate like a pig, so it was more like five children.

But unlike what people think, I stopped spending money left and right because I'm right-handed, so how can I spend it left?

## JANUARY 5

*Dear Diary:*

I went for a massage today at a new place. The old one sucked and I'm no longer interested in intercourse. I need a different kind of release.

All I require these days is some finger poking.

I love meeting new people, so when the new masseuse greeted me, I said, "What's your name?"

She said, "Jessica."

I said, "Nice to meet you, Jessica. Do you wanna know my name?"

She said, "No."

We walked into a dark room, and Jessica told me to put my face in a hole. It was extremely dark, and I was unsure where the hole was, so I just jumped through Adam Lambert's gauges.

During the massage I was wondering what it takes to be a full-time masseuse. Do you have to be a top and to like poking people? In all seriousness, being a masseuse is exactly like being a chef. How? When I worked at a restaurant, I massaged so much kale on my very first day that kale finally stood up and tipped me ten bucks.

Since my culinary school was semi-vegetarian, I fell madly in love with kale. I say "semi" because the school included some meat action in the curriculum and, please, I'm a gay man, so I know a thing or two about handling meat. To be credited by the New York State, a culinary school must incorporate meat classes in its courses or otherwise they're unable to call themselves a real school. For gay men to be credited by the New York State, you must also get some meat action bi-weekly, or otherwise you can't call yourself gay.

## JANUARY 6

*Dear Diary:*

After reminiscing about my culinary school days, I briefly considered becoming a vegan again. When I lived in Denver, I was vegan for two years and loved how skinny I was. I'd even thrown out any leather product I had.

I love meat (obviously), but I love veggies more, especially french fries. I like eggplants and peaches (and eggplant and peach emojis), but am I prepared to throw out my leather belts again? Then how am I getting spanked?

Pre-vegan, I had a meaty, juicy, textbook bubble butt. After converting to veganism I lost forty pounds including my ass, and I received a pancake in its place. And you know what? Pancakes are for breakfast, but the boys are hungry all day long. So if I truly want a boyfriend I have to think bigger somehow.

And speaking of bigger; a bigger salary wouldn't hurt. Listen, you haven't lived until you've deep-throated a huge salary. Ask Kendra Wilkinson. Only in her case, she didn't call it a "huge" salary. She called it "Hugh's." She had a cock in her mouth for fuck's sake, so she couldn't pronounce things correctly.

## JANUARY 7

*Dear Diary:*

Today is Orthodox Christmas in Russia, akin to regular Christmas but not entirely. Nobody exchanges presents, Mariah Carey is not singing on the radio, and the bus runs on a weekday schedule.

But here what's strange: for the past week, the number "forty" keeps appearing in my life. I'll notice it in books, or someone's fortieth birthday would come up, or Angelina Jolie would adopt her fortieth child.

I'm not a big believer in reading signs, but this hardly seems like a coincidence. Apparently, in the Bible, the number forty appears a hundred and forty-six times—I counted! I even counted the number of partners I've had, and it's also forty (per month).

Day forty this year falls on February ninth. Will I die prematurely before I even start ejaculating prematurely? I'm only thirty-one, for fuck's sake. In an ordinary world, that is, but I live in a gay one, so I'm four hundred years old: Betty White's age and Queen Elizabeth's.

The good news is in dog years, I'm barely four!


## JANUARY 8

*Dear Diary:*

I went for a run at the gym. Unlike most people I know, I love cardio and running. I abuse my gym membership more than I abuse my stomach during the holidays. Even more than Amy Winehouse abused cocaine.

Exercising is essential in my world. In one day, I could exercise three to four to five times. Only by then, I don't call it "exercising." I call it a "threesome."

## JANUARY 9

*Dear Diary:*

Two weeks ago, there was an explosion at the ConEdison plant in Astoria. I was so frightened, Diary, like a real sissy boy. This was written in a local newspaper: "The entire sky turned blue for three minutes, and you could see the 'blue mushroom' from space."

First of all, who is "you"? Most people I know live in New York, and we don't have "space" here.

Second of all, why does it matter whether anybody saw the "blue mushroom" from space? Who is there to watch? It's not like we have a colony on Mars and they all collected outside in their suits and watched the ConEdison explosion. So what? Will they dial the Earth right away and say, "Hey, is everything OK? Is there a nuclear war?" The Martians would hang up thinking, "Well, we don't fucking care. We don't live there anymore."

Besides, a *blue* mushroom? Are we having an explosion or ayahuasca?

When the explosion happened everyone thought aliens were attacking us, and by everyone, I mean a hookup who was over that evening.

The very last time I assumed aliens were attacking me, I was rolling high on Molly and called everyone in my phone book at four o'clock in the morning. Nobody picked up and I was appalled! Nobody speaks on the phone anymore—that's why I'm appalled. Even the debt collectors stopped calling. They text me from a number I don't recognize, *"Sup, bitch?"*

At least, I think they're debt collectors because they always follow up with, *"What's your address again?"* Or *"Send me pictures of your broke ass."*

## JANUARY 10

*Dear Diary:*

I work as an office manager for a startup, and the company has developed a "visual scale" but it's not for sale yet. The scale is a camera that scans your body and speaks your exact weight out loud. It's insanely accurate. Just today, when I walked in, the scale yelled, "Fat!"

After work, I went for a happy hour with my annoying friend, Justin. First, I don't understand why they call it a happy hour when it lasts five and a half. And second, I don't understand why my friend calls himself Justin when his real name is Justin-And-A-Half.

Maybe in the good old days a happy hour lasted an actual hour, just like Justin's complaining. "I'm so fat! I will never have a boyfriend! I wish I were straight!"

On and on and on. Well, you won't find a boyfriend with that attitude, bitch! Louis Armstrong may have started his famous quote with "It's a small step for a man," but he ended it with, "it's a giant leap for mankind."

I'm unsure how the saying fits, but I'll use every trick up my sleeve to shut the bitch up.

## JANUARY 11

*Dear Diary:*

I'm embarrassed! Louis Armstrong has never said the above quote. Louis just blew in his trumpet, while Neil Armstrong was the one who flew to the moon.

One blew—one flew. Who knew?

Diary, will people get outraged that I compared two people who sound so similar? Millions of people have the same name, and it's hard for me to keep track of everyone. Is it Bush Sr., Bush Jr., or Jessica Simpson's bush? Who can even tell the difference?

By the way, there will always be two of everything: the Olsen twins, a twosome, or double penetration.


## JANUARY 12

*Dear Diary:*

Six days left before my surgery. What if the surgery is botched and I end up looking like Jocelyn Wildenstein? Or worse, like Jocelyn Wildenstein at eight in the morning as soon as she wakes up? Or even worse, like Jocelyn Wildenstein looking in a mirror of Jocelyn Wildenstein?

I started looking at my old photos and reminiscing about my gay old life (I'm gay, which is why my life is gay. Makes sense?). I love going down memory lane.

Do you think after the surgery Judge Judy will allow me to change my name to Skinny Bitch? She'll ask me why I wanna rename myself to Skinny Bitch, and I'll just purse my lips, swing my hips, and point at my new, skinny face. Judge Judy will nod and say, "What would prompt you to do something so stupid?"

Last year, Macaulay Culkin polled his fans, asking whether he should change his name to Macaulay Macaulay Culkin Culkin. This obsession with everything double must stop. Walk into any McDonald's and order the double cheeseburger. Then cross the street to another McDonald's and order the double-fried chicken.

What's next? A thirty-dollar cocktail because they double froze my ice cubes?

Emily Blunt used to stutter but she never had a dumb idea to call herself Emily Emily Blunt Blunt. Double is over. Ask Cher or Adele—the shorter the better. Unless you talk about penises. Then it's the opposite.

## JANUARY 13

*Dear Diary:*

I hate my life right now for a variety of reasons: I'm constipated, I need some penetration (it's been at least two days), and I have a dozen bills to pay. That's why I'm bitter today—the bills.

I took out a twenty-one-thousand-dollar loan to attend a culinary school. For the next twelve months, I paid four thousand toward the loan, thinking my balance would be seventeen thousand upon graduating. A year later, my balance was higher than when I started because of the interest. I was like, "This is bullshit!"

I just wish I'd known about such shady business. Listen, bitch, if I need shade I'll sit by the pool with a drink under an umbrella or fly to London where there's no sun.

## JANUARY 14

*Dear Diary:*

I hate my commute. I've lived in Astoria, Queens, for over a decade, and I've just realized I've spent nine full months on the subway. Nine months! I could have had a fucking baby by now, or a college degree, but did I get any diploma? No, just a blow job in a dark alley on Thirtieth Avenue.

Besides, I'm hungover and depressed. I went out last night to drown my sorrows because my boss makes me miserable. He's gay, skinny, and handsome—a dangerous combination when you're young and rich. My job as an office manager includes market research, ordering snacks, and greeting potential (mostly gay) investors who are interested in our "visual scale." Appearance is critical, but yesterday my boss said, "Why is your face so pudgy before my meeting? Go and plunge it into a bucket of ice water and douche. I need you to weigh five pounds lighter by ten!"

## JANUARY 15

*Dear Diary:*

In three days I'll have my surgery, and hopefully my boss will stop saying I'm fat. Do you think afterward, when Dr. Michael Swango removes buccal fat from my face, I'll get a boyfriend (or at least a meaningful hookup)? Or will the surgery change nothing?

Perhaps I'm as unlikable as a piece of bacon at a bar mitzvah. I work with Jewish people and I'm confused because half of them eat bacon, and a quarter of them don't. Well, half of them are vegetarian, and a quarter is not, so maybe that's why.

Sorry, my math skills suck, and why wouldn't they? Like Daddy, like his skills.

## JANUARY 16

*Dear Diary:*

I went to my primary care doctor for a checkup. Everything is fine, but it's been so long since the last checkup that I needed someone to touch my balls. I asked Dr. Harry Bush for a blood test to learn my blood type, so he ordered it. But he also said I shouldn't worry, and if I ever need a blood transfusion, they'll order three liters of cold brew from Starbucks. He's *so* rude. Who fucking drinks Starbucks?

## JANUARY 17

*Dear Diary:*

I made a mistake by telling Bagwis that I'm paying six thousand dollars tomorrow for my surgery. Bagwis is Filipino, and his name means "long feather" in Tagalog.

He said, "What would prompt you to do something so stupid?"

I said, "I need a boyfriend."

He rolled a joint and said, "Don't waste your money. Go to South America and get it done there for cheaper, and you'll have a vacation out of it."

He's so dumb. Is he a "long feather" or "long in the tooth"?

I rolled my eyes and said, "Then what? When I return to New York, I'm all botched, and that scares me. If I want something scary, I'll watch Kelly Osbourne's liposuction on YouTube."

By the way, anything that starts with the letter "K" is scary to me. Kremlin, karma, kayak. That's right; a kayak is *scary*. Listen, if I must swim in a long, hollow tree, I'll just swim in Khloé Kardashian.

## JANUARY 18

*Dear Diary:*

Today is a busy day for me. Dr. Michael Swango is removing fat from my cheeks in the evening after work, and he's already prescribed me some oxy, which I'd picked up from the pharmacy on the way to work and had one for fun.

Dr. Michael Swango said I must be on a liquid diet for the next few days and prohibited me from putting anything solid in my mouth.

"Like what?" I asked.

"Like an erect penis."

"That's a massive problem for a gay man, doctor."

"Figure it out."

While on oxy, I called the Viagra headquarters and asked if they could fax me a list of their most valuable customers—anyone who gets soft. Vicky from Viagra asked me to fax them my stats and torso pictures, and if a client was interested, Vicky would give me a call.

## JANUARY 19

*Dear Diary:*

The surgery went incredibly well, but I haven't been this swollen around the mouth since sucking an eleven-inch penis.

Listen, size matters and there's only so much room. I'm a New Yorker, for fuck's sake. Have you ever seen a grand piano in Astoria? No. Then why would there be an eleven-inch penis in my mouth? There's no room! Even if I get the piano in (or the penis), there are also two balls attached to it and a huge *bush*. At which point, it's not Astoria—it's *Bush*wick.


## JANUARY 20

*Dear Diary:*

Vicky from Viagra faxed me some names, so now I have options. There weren't many people on her list, but at least the Vatican priests were interested because they said I had a babyface.

You know what? I think I'll just take another oxy, two shots of tequila, and melatonin. True, I won't be awake for the high to come, but I want my unconsciousness to have some fun, too.


## JANUARY 21

*Dear Diary:*

My lab results came back and I finally learned my blood type: O positive, the most common (thirty-seven percent), which means the most valuable.

I *love* it! Everything has been negative in my life thus far, but now I know that I have lots of positive stuff going through my body, aside from oxy and martinis.

## JANUARY 22

*Dear Diary:*

I'm feeling depressed because my face is swollen and looks giant, so I'm too lazy to write much, but I must share what I overheard on the subway coming from work: "Everybody keeps saying it's gonna be four inches, five inches, or six inches. That's nothing. I'm from Chicago. Try ten inches!"

Tonight's snowstorm's got everyone talking like we're on Grindr!

## JANUARY 23

*Dear Diary:*

I made a cocktail with oxy, Benadryl, and stool softener, and got a little high. I even thought the storm was kind of amazing to watch. We barely got two inches in.

Then hot Rod pulled out and said, "I forgot I have to go home."

## JANUARY 24

*Dear Diary:*

I was distraught when hot Rod left too quickly last night. I took it personally. Was I not enough for him? But also, because I didn't cum, I was left alone to play with myself, so I pulled out some dildos. Yes, *some*. Plural.

I'm a gay man, so finding a sex partner should be reasonably straightforward, and yet here I am; playing by myself.

After taking oxy, I feel better. Who cares about hot Rod or my swollen mouth? The only thing I care about right now is a good lie to call out tomorrow.

The best lies and conspiracies involve the moon, 9/11, or the president. But I can't text my boss and say, *"I can't come to work because Trump is still the president."*

Later that night, while playing with my dildos, I came up with a good lie and emailed my supervisor, Bad Breath and Beyond: *"Good evening, Halitosis. I'm not coming in tomorrow. Is it just me, or is the snowstorm horrible? It's snowing so bad that I swear I just saw Whitney Houston on a bulldozer collecting all the snow."*


## JANUARY 25

*Dear Diary:*

I made a new cocktail with oxy, Tums, and Gas-X, and for some reason, the cocktail made me hungry. I assumed the new Ariana Grande's song "7 Rings" was about onion rings, so I ordered some online. In the lyrics, Ariana is having breakfast at Tiffany's.

Do you think they serve onion rings there? I'm calling to find out. Hold on . . .

Epic fail, Diary. I just got off the phone with Tiffany, who claims you can't make a reservation for months! Whatever, I'll go to Bareburger, then, instead.

So much for being classy, but after eating seven onion rings, at least I got gassy—but don't worry, the cocktail of oxy, Tums, and Gas-X helped.

## JANUARY 26

*Dear Diary:*

Since I'm still high on oxy, I saw an angel today. That's the name of the handyman at work. So I saw him.

What kind of name is Angel, anyhow? So unoriginal! There are many fun names in the Bible, like Apostle, the Arc, or Burning Bush.

Actually, Burning Bush is the name for me and my jock itch (except in my case, there's no jock; so just an itch).

## JANUARY 27

*Dear Diary:*

My oxy ran out. There's no more pain in my mouth, but I asked Dr. Michael Swango for a refill anyway.

I'm glad I keep a diary because oxy is a memory-eraser. After rereading what I'd written, I must clarify one thing: Ariana

Grande's song "7 Rings" was *not* about onion rings, and I have no idea what the hell she's saying.

What does "my neck is flossing" even mean?

Who cares? If I learned nothing else from *Pretty Woman*, at least I learned that flossing is essential.

**JANUARY 28**

*Dear Diary:*

Thanks to Ariana Grande and her song about flossing, I realized I should be more meticulous about my teeth. I drink cold brew coffee like my life depends on it, and as a result, my teeth are yellow. Since I had to pick up some stool softeners for myself, I stopped at the store and added some teeth-whitening strips to my basket.

Unfortunately, I drool so much that when I wore the first treatment, the bleaching solution dribbled out and bleached everything else around me—except my fucking teeth.

It wasn't a total waste, though: I dribbled on my whites and did laundry.

**JANUARY 29**

*Dear Diary:*

I got a haircut at a new place today and hate it. The hairstylist was too much *blah, blah, blah* and not enough *chop, chop, chop*.

Unlike other people, my face starts resembling a watermelon if my hair grows longer on the sides. So I asked the stylist to square them off, which she did and now I resemble SpongeBob.

Later that evening, when I came to the grocery store, a worker grabbed me and stuffed me on the shelf with sponges and dish-washing liquid. But I didn't mind.

I love getting stuffed.

## JANUARY 30

*Dear Diary:*

I was chatting with a cute boy on Grindr, and after about an hour, he told me I had a filthy mouth and should filter what I say. Leave me alone, bitch! I'm broke and can't afford a filter.

The truth is I like dirty talk: the dirtier, the better. Dirtier than Flushing and even dirtier than Anne Hathaway's armpits.

Think *much* dirtier.

Did you imagine the cast of *Jersey Shore*?

Sorry, but no; I said dirty, not trashy.

## JANUARY 31

*Dear Diary:*

My super Mario texted me today. Mario said he checked on my apartment while I was out and told me my windows needed treatment.

I was busy having a threesome, so I thought Mario meant that *I* needed treatment. Like for my jock itch? Or did Mario mean I should get a treat for myself?

To check all my boxes, I went to Tiffany's and bought myself a platinum diamond ring for one thousand dollars—in credit, naturally.

That's some royal treatment, bitch!

Even if the diamonds were microscopic and reminded me of my paycheck, I loved them. It's not about seeing but about believing, right? For instance, when people brag about themselves, swearing they have a "good heart," I take it at face value. Only people like Ted Bundy could crack open a person and see if their heart was "good."

So I believe the diamonds are in the ring and that's what matters. Ariana Grande had seven rings, but even if I only have one, it has *seven* invisible diamonds.

The best part about my ring is not the metal or even the diamonds, but the return policy, which is thirty days.

However, Tiffany warned me that if I finger someone and the ring gets lost, they won't accept the boy with the ring inside. Trying to remove the ring by myself sounded complicated—I'm not a fucking engineer—so I purchased a fingering insurance policy for an extra two hundred dollars.

January was a fun month! My face got thinner, my finger got bedazzled, but I'm still a little behind on making savings. It's OK.

Like they say in Vegas: better luck next time!

# FEBRUARY

Grindr Bio: Hi, guys my name's (Big) Ben and I'm visiting London for the first time—from Astoria, New York. I'm a delight. For hookups only! 190 centimeters, 50 kilograms, 25 years old.

**FEBRUARY 1**

*Dear Diary:*

This month I vow to start saving money. To prove I'm for real, I paid off four credit cards earlier this morning. Yoo-hoo. Actually, "paid off" is a little misleading: I transferred balances to other cards, which means no interest fees for six more months (which also means more money to spend for me).

I transfer more balances every month than I transferred STDs back in 2011 during my slutty days. It's OK. I'm a dreamer. Something big will come this year.

Update: something big did come today. My hookup today was twelve inches!


**FEBRUARY 2**

*Dear Diary:*

I spent a couple of hours on Craigslist today. I like to go on Craigslist at least once a month to confirm I'm not overpaying. I compare the square footage of nearby apartments, assess their prices, and adjust them for inflation.

Though, each rental listing is like a Donald Trump's tweet: all lies.

When the listing says, "The apartment is located two blocks away from the subway," it means the apartment is located two avenues, plus fifteen blocks away from the subway.

"Fifteen minutes from Central Park on the W Train" may be technically correct, but they mean fifteen minutes in a perfect world. But you don't live in a perfect world, bitch. You're taking the MTA.

"Laundromat across the street is open 24/7." That one is true, but have you ever woken up at three in the morning to wash your cum-stained sheets?

Apartment listings are as misleading as personal descriptions on Grindr: "Gut-renovated, washer and dryer in unit, close to the subway" is as real as "Hung, drug-free, top."

## FEBRUARY 3

*Dear Diary:*

I invited a couple of gay friends over for dinner. I graduated from culinary school and I'm obsessed with feeding people. I stuff them until they can barely walk and today I made juicy baby back ribs. The boys clearly enjoyed the ribs because they continued sucking on the sauce-drenched bones even after finishing all the meat.

After dinner (or what we called a threesome), we finished the night at a gay bar in Woodside called Sherlock Homos. We watched a drag contest where a friend of mine—Priscilla, the Cunt of the Desert—was one of the contestants. Fun name! If I were a drag queen, my name would be Ama Payda Nothin.

Back in 2012, I was Cleopatra for Halloween, and I felt so high wearing six-inch heels. But at the end of the night, a guy with eleven inches topped the cake—and me!

## FEBRUARY 4

*Dear Diary:*

A guy without a picture messaged me on Grindr. I hate blank profiles, but since I was desperate and protein-deficient, I replied.

He: *"Sup."*
Me: *"Any pictures?"*
He: *"I'm discrete."*
Me: *"Discrete means isolated. Do you mean discreet?"*

He followed up with a picture of a headless nude photo belonging on a Latino guy and a dick belonging on a horse. I screenshot his photo right away—for safekeeping. If he's as good at organizing as he is at spelling, chances are he'll lose the photo.

He: *"What are you doing?"*
Me: *"Writing a comedy novel."*
He: *"Tell me something funny."*

How rude! Like, I didn't ask him what kind of horse he was, much like I wouldn't ask a deli worker to see his meat or a delivery guy to see his package.

Me: *"Sure, I'll send you something funny."*

I sent him back his own picture.

He probably lost it between then and now, anyway.

He blocked me.

**FEBRUARY 5**

*Dear Diary:*

I went to a housewarming party for my chiropractor A-wut. This year I warm more houses than ConEdison and fireplaces combined. I always bring a small present and the cheapest bottle of wine to every party, and money is just draining and draining.

Or, rather, my credit card debt is just growing and growing...

After the initial chitchat and a few drinks, we started thinking about what games to play. The party was in Flatbush and Brookliners take their games seriously, so we played Jenga, Twister, and Spin the Bottom (when a bottom's ass turns towards you, you eat it).

The apartment was a hundred square feet for twenty people, and since A-wut didn't have room for any chairs, we sat on dildos. I'm glad I'd douched before we arrived.

Over all, a fun night!

**FEBRUARY 6**

*Dear Diary:*

Credit card companies are stupid. I'm bitter not only because I'm seventy thousand dollars in debt but also because their reward systems are confusing. I get five percent on groceries in January, but I get three on gas in March? I don't know anything about driving, and neither do I have a driver's license. What will these five percent net me in groceries? A sliver of a Kardashian?

First of all, am I supposed to eat food during one month but drink gas during another? I already take so much Gas-X it makes no sense, mathematically speaking, to add more gas to my system. I'm not a transformer (i.e., a versatile).

Plus, when I cook I peel my carrots and that's ten percent waste right there. Adding five percent cashback is no longer profitable.

Look, if you give rewards, reward me all year long like I reward guys while on my knees. I'm sick and tired of buying nine hundred liters of gas every March for five percent cashback.

(I sell it on the black market to make some pocket change.)

## FEBRUARY 7

*Dear Diary:*

There. Are. Zero. Single. Guys. On. The. Apps.

Guys chatting on Grindr are mainly couples looking for a third, a fourth, or a high. Even my former gym emailed me with, *"Join with no commitment."*

Nobody wants to commit anymore!

Coke's slogan "Open Happiness" explains why every gay man is an open relationship: They do too much coke. They also do lots of poppers but that's a much different story—a fisting one.

I also realized that Wendy's slogan "Where's the beef?" is not about Sam Smith's weight loss like I'd initially thought, but about my cheek fat.

Where's the beef you ask? It's all gone, bitch!

## FEBRUARY 8

*Dear Diary:*

Companies come up with other slogans and tag lines to target the gay community. Advertisers assume that gay men have money (which is true), and I'm convinced all the ads are for us.

Take the ad for California Milk Processor Board. It's simple: "Got milk?" That's the opening line to every message I send. Do you think that was not intentional?

BMW's slogan "Designed for driving pleasure" was also used by a dildo company, Dildos R Us. I purchased three dildos without even reading the online reviews.

But airlines are even more fly (see what I did there?) because they know the queer community loves traveling.

For instance, British Airways caters strictly to the BDSM "parTy" community: "To fly. To serve."

While Turkish Airlines is into fisting: "Widen your world."

I once took a plane to Turkey, and my ass wouldn't close for a week.

And every time I have sex, I quote TAM Airlines. I say, "I'm glad you came."

## FEBRUARY 9

*Dear Diary:*

Do you remember how back in January I complained about how number forty kept popping up everywhere? Well, today is day forty of 2019, but nothing horrendous happened to me or my anus! We didn't lose a leg, our vision is still 20/20, and we didn't get stretched in a weird way.

I'm a believer, and I wanna believe in signs, but thus far the only accurate signs are the subway signs: "Take the N Train if you wanna be late for work while smelling armpits and urine for thirty minutes."

## FEBRUARY 10

*Dear Diary:*

The whitening strips failed! They're like my brother: they refuse to work. Instead, I went to a dentist who professionally bleached my teeth for only six hundred dollars.

After the procedure I rushed to the bathroom and smiled. My smile was like lightning, and it brightened the whole room, almost blinding me. I had no idea I could be a fucking weapon! The FDA will be issuing a warning: "To avoid blindness, please wear SPF 30 sunscreen and sunglasses near this bad bitch."

After using the facilities, I returned to the doctor and told him, "I want my teeth bleached every month."

Dr. Canine said, "If you wanna spend your money and if you're stupid, sure. But if you drink your cold brew coffee through a straw, you never have to come back, bro!"

That's when it hit me why my teeth were so yellow to begin with: I never drink anything through a straw.

## FEBRUARY 11

*Dear Diary:*

To show off my newly bleached teeth, I went to have dinner with my best friend Bagwis. I haven't been to Hell's Kitchen in seven forevers and now I remember why: because of how crowded Hell's Kitchen is!

Not only was it crowded, but the zombies walking around barely looked in front of them. To avoid collisions, I had to maneuver around, duck, and jump. I haven't moved my head up and down that much since my last blow job.

What a nightmare.

When I finally made it to the Vietnamese restaurant, the line was curving around the block, and it took thirty minutes and a Britney song before we sat down.

I was annoyed. Listen, I'm twenty-one thousand dollars in debt from culinary school, so I know how to create cohesive meals. I could've made us a similar noodle dish at home for cheaper and I would only charge Bagwis twelve bucks. At my home restaurant, the wait time for a table is seven minutes flat. Unless you have a big dick, then it's five.

I've been trying to save money for some time now, but where is it all going? It's not like I'm spending it left and right.

## FEBRUARY 12

*Dear Diary:*

I've just booked a flight to London, and it will be my very first time! Since nobody goes to London in February (because it's cold) the roundtrip tickets cost me five hundred dollars, while the hotel for four days came out to another five hundred. I saved two thousand dollars by not booking my trip last minute. Plus, I saved ten thousand dollars by not flying to Hawaii. Cha-Ching! Don't tell me I don't know how to save money.

**FEBRUARY 13**

*Dear Diary:*

Can't wait until I'm old. I want people to offer me their seat when I take the subway (which won't happen in New York). Listen, when a ninety-year-old grandma enters the subway, nobody will offer her a seat, and she'll be standing until someone shuts off the oxygen tank she's carrying with her.

We used to give up seats for the elderly and pregnant women. But now? I'm afraid to give up my seat to anyone, because people get offended and defensive, like, "How old do you think I am, bitch?"

Since New York is out for me, I'm contemplating retiring somewhere gay, so probably not Afghanistan. Don't get me wrong, I enjoy looking at their black, red, and green flag, but that pattern doesn't go well with "fabulous"—what I like to wear. (Did you know that while homosexuality is illegal in Afghanistan, they have something called *bacha bazi*, which is when uber-wealthy older men have young boys dance for them and do sexual favors? Such double standards!)

In Russia, Putin signed into federal law that discussing LGBT issues with minors is punishable by imprisonment. Similarly, Putin's wife (Donald Trump) is taking us that route, too. When two delusional negatives meet each other—Putin and Trump—mathematically speaking, they must cancel each other out, right? Like when two negatives create a positive, like two bottoms create a top, or like two Renée Zellwegers create a tight facelift.

## FEBRUARY 14

*Dear Diary:*

Today is Valentine's Day, so fuck, fuck, fuck everyone. I'm depressed, and when I'm depressed I eat and drink. I made a small shopping list of only three items: seventeen cakes, a shipping container of potato chips, and a case of vodka.

Valentine's Day is not for single people because everything at the buffet is heart-shaped when you shop for lunch. It's not like on Presidents' Day cooks shape every food item into the president (I never saw a cupcake shaped like Barack Obama back in 2009) and it's not like every Memorial Day we only talk about memory loss and Alzheimer's. We just can't take holidays so literally.

Although, wait a second—I'm lying. Some holidays I take literally. For instance, I forgot that on one Groundhog Day I went to Pennsylvania, knocked on the groundhog's door, and said, "Hey, Harvey Weinstein, you hairy asshole, what's up?"

## FEBRUARY 15

*Dear Diary:*

Saw a man on the train reading a book. I love it when other people read. I always wave at them, and if they pretend not to notice me, I'll sit next to them and start a conversation or loudly fart.

However, this man farted first, so I took a look at the title of his book: "Irritable Bowel Syndrome. Diverticulitis."

Great book—I've read it, too! I thought it was a quick bathroom read.

**FEBRUARY 16**

*Dear Diary:*

Do you remember how I started drinking my coffee through a straw to avoid staining my teeth? Well, guess what? The State of California has banned plastic straws, and the same fate is awaiting New York in two years.

The activists who made that happen claim that plastic straws are not recyclable, which is a total surprise to me. Aren't they plastic, as in a "plastic" straw?

The straws, apparently, also pollute our oceans. On top of that, some sea turtles eat the straws and die. Why would anyone in their right mind eat a straw? The turtles must be stupid or desperate. Besides, if they're so-called "sea" turtles, what the fuck are they doing in the ocean?

So now what? I don't wanna be responsible for killing whales (or was it turtles? I can't even remember). I went online and ordered myself reusable metal straws with silicone tips, and they'll arrive in two days.

Later that day, I read an article, from which I quote: "Ordering from the internet plays a major role in fossil fuel emissions."

Ugh!

I'm lost trying to figure out what's right and what's wrong or who's the top and who's the bottom. From now on, anything goes, and it's every queen for herself!

Anyway, the metal straws I purchased will help me save some money in the long run. It's a win-win for the turtles and me.

Except, fuck the turtles. So just me.

## FEBRUARY 17

*Dear Diary:*

I'm genuinely proud of myself for saving four hundred dollars on clothes today. I didn't purchase any. I also didn't buy a new laptop from Apple that cost two thousand or another ring from Tiffany's for one thousand. I saved enough dough for a down payment on a house and promptly took myself out to dinner to celebrate.

## FEBRUARY 18

*Dear Diary:*

Today is Presidents' Day, and we're supposed to celebrate our current president, Donald Trump. I was wrong on Valentine's Day about one thing: everything in stores today, from cakes to muffins, is shaped like a toupee. Even the lights atop the Empire State Building showcased a unique orange hue to honor Trump's tan he'd acquired on yet another golf retreat in Florida that we, the taxpayers, must recompense.

On a positive note: my metal straws arrived, and I'm happy to start saving children (or was it turtles? Can't remember). And not just the turtles! I wanna protect birds, too. So for dinner, I ordered a steak and not poultry.

See? I'm clogging my arteries just to save a few chickens. I'm so fucking selfless.

## FEBRUARY 19

*Dear Diary:*

I consider it strange that while there are dozens of countries in the continent of "America" (like Mexico, Canada, or especially *Colombia*), we are the only "Americans," while they are Mexicans, Canadians, or *poor*.

Was it rude of me to say Colombia was poor? Last time when I dined at a Colombian restaurant, they served me only half a chicken, and I like things in wholes—ask my dates.

## FEBRUARY 20

*Dear Diary:*

I got my second haircut this year and I hate it. The hairdresser robbed me! Not my money—but all my hair is gone! I look like Mr. Clean but short, skinny, and dirty. The hairdresser, whose name is Asshole, talked nonstop for the entire hour and didn't let me get a word in edgewise.

How will I look Londoners in the eye tomorrow and quote Adele, "Hello, it's me"? How will I hook up when my hairy carpet doesn't match the bald drapes? And worst of all, how will I face the Queen?

I emailed her right away, *"Liz, I cunt go to London like this."*

She emailed back, *"You cun, hun!"*

I'll never cut my hair again—or at least not until next month. I'm even willing to resemble a hairy Chewbacca (as long as I stay short, skinny, and cute).

Seriously, though, what was Asshole's obsession with cutting off. Every. Single. Hair. On. My. Head?

Am I getting a haircut or a fucking Brazilian?

## FEBRUARY 21

*Dear Diary:*

I'm on an overnight flight to London. I've never visited Europe before, so I purchased a book of manners from a JFK book store.

Apparently, in London Big Ben is what they call Ben Affleck. The British call him "Big" Ben because his penis is longer in centimeters. He's only five inches in California, but he's known as "Big Ben with a Long Shlong" in the UK.

That means my penis is also longer, and I can barely wait to insert it in places it doesn't belong. Like inside a 220-volt electricity socket or someone's mouth.

I'm also much higher in the UK—from *five* feet to a *hundred and eighty* centimeters, which means I won't need any poppers to get higher.

In London, when you talk about money, you talk about pounds, right? But when you talk about pounds, you talk about stones. So confusing!

I don't know how much I weigh in stones, but in "brick" I'm a three-story building. In fact, in London I weigh one-eighth of the Shard.

**FEBRUARY 22**

*Dear Diary:*

I just took a Piccadilly line to Cockfosters on the Tube. It's London, bitch! Straight up, I went sight-seeing and crossed more bridges than I crossed my eyes while taking the subway in New York.

British people are obsessed with misspelling stuff. For the longest time, I thought it was Down*town* Abbey, but it's Down*ton* Abbey. I also thought it was West*minister* Abbey (or at least West*mister* Abbey), but it's actually West*minster* Abbey.

Last, I learned the apartment where Liz lives is called the Buckingham Palace, but have you seen the royal family tree? They multiply faster than a virus, and the palace ought to be renamed to the Fuckingam Palace. The line for the throne is longer than the line at Trader Joe's.

It sounds like I'm venting, but I wouldn't mind living there at all. At the Fuckingham Palace, I mean. Listen, I'm a gay man, and sex is vital to me, kind of like misspelling is vital to British people.

The British only misspell to avoid sounding like us. After all, they had Jersey and Hampshire first, until we stole them and renamed them to Smelly Shore and A State You Can't Find On The Map.

Did you know the British used to speak like the Americans, but once they realized we'd stolen their town names and language, they adopted an accent? Who got independence from whom, you start wondering. The British are so industrious that they hate to be like everyone else. Now they're even Brexiting to prove their point.

I love history, and I hope visiting where the Americans come from will help me appreciate the U.S. better.

My first stop in London: a pub!

## FEBRUARY 23

*Dear Diary:*

London: pubs, PUBS everywhere.

My bedroom: pubes, PUBES everywhere.

I guess the British are not the only ones who like to misspell stuff! London is fabulous, though. I did more sight-seeing, but I still must cross another three hundred bridges. Do you know that stupid song about the London Bridge? It goes like, "London Bridge is falling down, my fair lady."

Why is it falling down? Did it try going down on another bridge first and realized its knees were hurting? That's so not gay. If your knees are hurting, put a pillow under them. And also, isn't it technically politically incorrect to call someone a "fair lady"? If you're pale with red hair, don't call yourself a fair lady. Call yourself Irish.

Hyde Park is clean, green, and gorgeous—after you find it. It's a British game called Hyde and Seek. In the gay world, it's called Hide Your Seed.

After lunch, I went to the Tate museum and learned it was an "imposing art gallery" (whatever that means). The Tate is a spinoff from a strip club called the Tit in Boise, Ohio. Our countries are similar on so many levels!

## FEBRUARY 24

*Dear Diary:*

Still in London. I insulted a cute guy today at the supermarket. I told him to suck my cock, and he's like, "I don't eat meat—I'm a vegetarian." Vegetarian, schmegetarian. What a queen! So picky. In my day, there were no vegetarian eaters, paleo eaters, or asshole eaters.

Growing up in Soviet Russia, my mom expected me to finish everything she placed in front of me. We lived in Siberia, and our cuisine was all over the place. So when we couldn't afford chicken, we made dumplings with cats. The only problem with cat meat is that you start shedding and taking lots of naps. The only person who truly enjoyed cat meat was Alec N. Wildenstein.

I mean, I respect alternatives to pork, chicken, and beef, like tofu, beans, or cats. But if you wanna save the planet (or your money) starving is not the answer. Ask Paris Hilton if she saved anyone lately by starving.

I rest my case.

## FEBRUARY 25

*Dear Diary:*

While having my fifth serving of fish and chips in London, I was chatting on Snapchat about diets with Bagwis.

He said he was going on a diet to lose some weight, but here's the catch: if he wants to eat something, he must make it from scratch. So if he wants cookies, he must shop at Food Bazaar International, make the dough in his pink KitchenAid, and then bake them.

Such a diet sounds smart as I like the idea of working for my food. Listen, I can milk a guy for hours just to get fed. However, making cookies or fish and chips is easy, but what if I want some penne Bolognese? Do I have to kill, chop, and grind some beef? Perhaps when I'm back in New York I should give it a go for a week. So what if I kill a few cows along the way? My weight is more important than saving an udder or two. Plus cow farts are killing the planet, with each producing five hundred pounds of methane per year, which causes the greenhouse effect. Temperatures are rising. By eating more beef, I'm risking a heart attack just so New Yorkers stay cool in the summer. That's a great patriot (said he humbly).

For dinner I had a beef Wellington, a shepherd's pie, and for dessert, Eton Mess. Bagwis texted me and said it got colder in New York and my plan of cooling the planet is working! After dinner I went to Soho and played some *putt-putt*, and back at the hotel, drunk and horny, I played with my *butt-butt*.

## FEBRUARY 26

*Dear Diary:*

Flew back to New York today.

London was fabulous and all, but if I see fish and chips one more fucking time...

They're served *everywhere*. Have the British heard of something called a salad? It's that green stuff sticking out from a gay man's mouth in Soho.

Also, why are people in London obsessed with the Queen? Have the British heard of something called a drag queen? It's that loud bitch a gay man tips in Soho.

Last, about those yellow teeth—have the British heard of something called a dentist? It's that woman in a white coat who's drilling a gay man's tooth in Soho . . .

Sorry, I don't mean anything I said. I'm venting because I'm tired, cranky, and most importantly, sex-deprived. I couldn't get lucky for some reason. British men don't find me attractive, I guess. Or maybe they think my mouth had become too small to accommodate their eighteen-centimeter schlongs after my surgery.

For instance, I chatted with a guy who avoided sleeping with tourists because he wants a steady dick. Ugh! Such a queen. When he wants a long, moist blow job, he sticks his schlong into a piece of chicken pot pie.

Last night at three in the morning, a tourist, like me, came over—clearly desperate for sex, same as me. He was cute, young, and Polish. After I polished him off, though, he wouldn't leave my hotel room for hours, trying to talk and connect and cuddle. Eye roll.

He didn't need a hookup. He needed a shrink.

Harry Styles eventually left when I said, "I want a relationship with you," which worked like magic.

## FEBRUARY 27

*Dear Diary:*

I returned my diamond ring to Tiffany's today. Tiffany asked me what was wrong.

What was *wrong*? Was she crazy? Was Tiffany that oblivious that she failed to see through my pathetic life?

So I told her what was wrong: "I'm upset because I feel like a fat slob after my vacation in London where I ate nothing but greasy fish and chips. I still don't have a boyfriend and I couldn't even get a simple hookup! I hate my job, I hate my debt, and I hate the fact I don't have any savings. We haven't impeached Donald Trump—"

Tiffany interrupted me and said, "I don't mean what's wrong with your personal life. What the fuck is wrong with the ring, bitch?"

"That makes more sense, Tiff. The ring is now too small. After my vacation, my fingers got incredibly swollen, and the word 'sausage' does not begin to describe them."

Tiffany smiled and said, "Your fingers are fine, ho. The hole in the ring had become smaller."

"Bless your heart."

"To make the hole bigger, you must relax and take some poppers."

Sorry, Diary, I got distracted and accidentally wrote the message I just tried to send on Grindr.

Anyhow, Tiffany suggested resizing the ring to make it bigger. First of all, how do you stretch a metal ring? Does it expand in boiling water like pasta?

On the other hand, resizing the ring might be the key to getting rich. I'd paid one thousand dollars, right? But if the hole grows bigger, so will the diamonds!

"Tiffany," I said, "grow the ring to fit an elephant or Mike Myers, and I'll keep it."

"Yeah, bitch, it ain't gonna happen."

So unfortunately, I went home empty-handed.

In the end, it wasn't a total loss of a subway fare. In a nearby neighborhood, Hudson Yards, I attended a fetish night at a sleazy gay bar, The Swallow, and if you want your hole resized, it was the night to do it.

**FEBRUARY 28**

*Dear Diary:*

OMG!

I just learned that Tiffany has been dead for months! Or at least weeks. So whoever served me last night at Tiffany's was one rude imposter! But whoever I served last night at The Swallow was one lucky pastor. I mean, he said he was a pastor, but he could have been lying, you know? Like, I always lie, for example, and tell people that I'm not in debt, that I have abs, and that my hole is tight.

# MARCH

**MARCH 1**

*Dear Diary:*

After getting paid yesterday, I sent the rent check to my landlady, had two drinks at a local bar, and now there are nine hundred dollars to my name. I must pay the creditors with the leftover money, pay for the utilities, and pay to get my nails done.

I'm so broke that I can barely afford food this month. So for lunch I went to suck a dick because it was cheap, healthy, and even Mom-approved. She always wanted me to eat more protein.

**MARCH 2**

*Dear Diary:*

I needed a synonym for an "old woman." Not sure why. Maybe I saw my face in the mirror.

Anyhow, the following words came up: witch, bitch, and hag. So rude! I'd never call Ivana Trump a hag, much like I'd never call Goldie Hawn a witch, much like I'd never call Elphaba a bitch. Wait, reverse that.

For comparison, I looked up a synonym for "an old man": beloved, fancy, and gigolo. I thought the disparity was quite striking and misogynist. Bruce Willis may be beloved, but I wouldn't say the opposite of that was "witch." Unfair! But that's the world we live in today: older women are bitches and hags, and older men grab pussies and become presidents.

On the other hand, at least I have something to look forward to when I get old—can't wait to be called "fancy." Will my pants be called "fancy pants"?

## MARCH 3

*Dear Diary:*

Watched movies with my ugly friend Spencer and we saw *Beauty and Spencer*. I mean, *Beauty and the Beast*. I realized the movie is not only about a cunt with zero fashion sense who falls in love with Boris Johnson, the movie is also about how you look at night (beauty) versus how you look in the morning (beast). But some of us always look ratchet. Right, Benedict Cumberbatch?

Any excess water retains in the face during the night, causing puffiness, and it's all because of gravity. Once you're up, gravity will eventually pull the water back down, but it can take hours. So I never let people see me in the morning until I finish five miles on a treadmill, shower, and plunge my face into a bucket of ice water to shrink pores. All these steps accelerate the depuffing process.

(PS, Andrew Breitbart, what's your excuse? Does water *ever* come down from your face? I guess not.)

After the ice water bucket, I use eye cream, a toner, a serum, a moisturizer, a mattifier, and sunscreen with SPF 45, followed by three different hair products: a thickener, a styling pomade, and hairspray. Then I proceed to the closet and spend an hour picking the perfect outfit.

My coworker Hung still wonders why I'm late. He would often ask something similar to, "Where were you at eight-thirty in the morning? That's when a person was murdered on Avenue C."

If I stood before the grand jury, and the jury asked me whether I killed Matt Doormat at eight-thirty on Tuesday morning, I would say, "Come again? *Killed*? It's before nine, and I didn't have any coffee, so if Matt Doormat came over at eight-thirty, then yes, I killed him."

**MARCH 4**

*Dear Diary:*

During my lunch break, I listened to a song by Cascada, a European singer who needs a breast-reduction surgery—just my opinion. The song was about cheating, and Cascada picked up a snooty, unpleasant tone and was singing off-tune—again, my opinion, "You cheated on me from behind."

Cascada is clearly not a gay man because "from behind" is a fantastic and *very* classy position. I heard even the Queen likes it. A local Astoria drag queen, that is, whose name is Sharon Pussies.

And once Chicago, my ex's Boston Terrier, humped my leg from behind and it felt as natural as douching. Even Ted Bundy's victims were singing, "You stabbed me from behind," because Ted Bundy was fucking classy.

## MARCH 5

*Dear Diary:*

I read an article today called: "The Most Googled Health Symptom in New York State." I called my best friend Bagwis to see what he thought the symptom was.

He said, "Definitely anal itching."

"I didn't ask about your symptoms. I said the whole state."

"Oh, the whole state? Then definitely anal itching."

"No, the answer is the loss of sleep."

Bagwis said, "Well, why do you think that is? They can't sleep because of their anal itching!"


## MARCH 6

*Dear Diary:*

I lost some weight! I was a hundred and sixty pounds this morning, but after shredding ten credit cards and douching, it went down to a hundred and fifty. Now it's on par with my credit score. When the pounds go down, the score goes up! (That's just good trigonometry.)


## MARCH 7

*Dear Diary:*

I was grocery shopping at Food Bazaar International and there was this annoying queen ahead of me in line. After bagging his groceries, the cashier asked him, "Credit?"

The queen seemed appalled. "Ugh," he said, "I heard 'Credit?' three times already and it's not even noon!"

Why was he yelling at the cashier? Was he tired of hearing the word "credit" for the third time? Then don't go shopping, bitch. Simple. Nobody is twisting your hairy arm! Plus, he's such an amateur, complaining about something so trivial. Try to come up with an excuse to call out while getting double penetrated while baking a sponge cake. Now that's something to complain about! Baking. Is. So. Fucking. Hard.

**MARCH 8**

*Dear Diary:*

Today is International Women's Day, which we don't celebrate in the United States for whatever misogynist reason.

To celebrate my favorite international chef—Giada's De Laurentiis—I purchased some Gas-X as I knew her Brussels sprouts would make me gassy. Thanks for the fart-fest in advance, Giada!

I love supporting other immigrants (like myself) and especially international women. Today, I don't even mind Melania Trump, who is Serbian or Slovakian or Slovenian. Who the fuck cares?

Did you know Slovenia is known for its caves? The caves are full of stalactites. Is it stalactites or stala*titties*? There are also stalagmites, but what kind of mites they are, I don't know. But they're not pubic hair mites.

Slovenia is also known for its bears and I'm a gay man, so I love my bears, especially if they're international—because they're uncircumcised.

## MARCH 9

*Dear Diary:*

This morning, the subway car was full of Swarovski crystals ads. The ads were irritating because they failed to resonate with me, their potential customer.

The first one was: "The act of giving is a gift in itself."

Is it? Then how come every time Monica Lewinsky gives a blow job it doesn't feel like a gift, but feels like impeachment? Or why every time I give a boyfriend the key to my apartment and wanna go steady, I never see him again?

The second ad: "Everyone should get a little something special."

Should they, though? Everyone? *Really?*

If by something special you mean herpes, then sure. If you mean Ebola, then no, thanks. That's too special.

The last ad: "Naughty or Nice—who's keeping score?"

Who's keeping score? Well, bitch: Santa, for one.

Have the Swarovski marketing team ever bowled? The machine keeps the score automatically!

I honestly think I should work in an advertising agency because I understand people's needs (listen, I'm on my knees way before anyone asks for it. That's just good customer service on my part). I would revamp the ads mentioned above and try reaching the correct (note: gay) demographic.

"The act of giving is a gift in itself—but take some poppers before you try your first fist."

"Naughty or Nice—who's keeping score? Just wash your hands upon using the restroom, and don't forget to stick your penis into my makeshift glory hole."

"If you won't buy our crystals, then what else are you gonna bedazzle on your dress? Dildos, bitch?"

## MARCH 10

*Dear Diary:*

My friend Jeffrey Dahmer asked me to water his plants while he's studying at a Columbia Correctional Institution in Portage, Wisconsin. Jeffrey is so rude. What next? Vacuum the carpet and cook you dinner? Clean out the freezer and bury the body? No, thanks.

When I helped him last time I almost tripped on a noose and twisted my ankle. I'm thirty-one, for fuck's sake. I can't be running around without my walker doing favors for people and kneeling without hurting my back. If you want a favor, Jeffrey, I'm all ears, but there better be something in it for me: cash, a hard dick, or a cheesecake.


## MARCH 11

*Dear Diary:*

I heard people on the internet (note: my real friends) were naming their genitalia, and I wanna weigh in on the action. I'm naming my penis Truth, which sounds like a rich person's name. Truth has a nice ring to it, and if there's Prince Albert attached to it, then there's an actual ring on it. If my penis were named Truth, I could finally tell my stupid coworker Hung when he asks me something stupid, "I'm gonna give you the Truth, but it'll be hard to swallow."

## MARCH 12

*Dear Diary:*

I'm proud of my diet, and the numbers on my scale are finally going down! I made another salad for lunch. My coworker Hung looked at a piece of red onion sticking out of my mouth and said, "How can you possibly eat a whole raw onion like that? You're such a savage."

Relax, drama queen. First of all, it was one slice.

I told him, "Listen, Urine-Colored Pants, I'm gonna give you the Truth, but it'll be hard to swallow."

He said, "Huh?"

I said, "Suck my dick!"

## MARCH 13

*Dear Diary:*

My thoughts are all over the place. One day I hate hooking up and want a relationship, and the following day I love hooking up and thrilled to have sex with multiple people—at once.

Now that the buccal fat is no longer in my mouth, people just wanna stuff my mouth with their fat shlongs.

To feel better, I always talk to myself in baby-talk. I'm unsure whether the baby talk is adult behavior, but I'd use just about anything to lift my spirits or lift my legs.

I'm annoyingly bipolar today, and I feel like I'm flip-flopping all over the place. Flip-flopping is only good if you're versatile but I'm not. I don't wanna wait until I'm sixty-nine (or until I'm in the sixty-nine position) before knowing what I want from my life.

I'm even unsure whether I want a doggie or a hot doggie. One sheds everywhere and the other one turns you into a pig.

I was distraught. To feel better, I took some oxy left over from my surgery because I wanted a high. Don't fucking judge me! I'm just a good Democrat, Diary, and take everything that Michelle Obama says seriously. So when I go low, I go high.

## MARCH 14

*Dear Diary:*

Yesterday—while on oxy—I thought it would be funny to invent a new ice cream flavor: "Lubed and Ribbed-for-His-Pleasure Condom."

Listen, I went to culinary school and I know how to make decent ice cream. When Donald Trump became president, I made ice cream with an imPEACH flavor in his honor. For FLOTUS—Mrs. Duck Lips—I made ice cream that tasted like Slovenia and fake tits. And for Ivanka I made French-style ice cream that tasted like donkeys, as I knew she'd appreciate something Jared.

Sorry, I'm being British and misspelled that—something *Jaded*.

## MARCH 15

*Dear Diary:*

I'm penniless. When my poppers wholesaler—Roger Stone—called me to borrow twenty bucks to buy himself two bras (in which he smuggles my poppers), I said, "You want two bras, Roger? Here you go: a-bra-cad-a-bra."

For real; if I continue being broke like this, for Christmas my friends can expect rocks from the beach, leaves from the trees, or me on my knees.

My bills are so high I think they hang out with Cheech & Chong way too often. Forget Cheech & Chong, I need to buy a new jockstrap and a thong. Until I can afford them I have to walk around commando, and my ass is freezing!

Lucy Ricardo was correct in wondering why money always marries money. Marry a broke guy for once! Do you know what I'd do if I married someone rich? I'd kill my husband, ask Carole Baskin how to bury the body, and invest his estate money into my passion!

Cooking. Not sucking cock.

I'd email my favorite chef Giada De Laurentiis (we're real close) and ask her if she wanted a new show, in which she makes the dough in front of the camera and I count the dough behind it.

**MARCH 16**

*Dear Diary:*

Today I attended a housewarming party in White Plains, Queens, for my white, plain friend Steven, a guy I once met on Fire Island. It was more of an orgy, but you catch my drift.

People had so much to eat . . . salads to toss and sausages to swallow. A toolbox on the kitchen table threw me off at first, but I was happy a lesbian was coming to fix an office chair we accidentally broke during a wild spit roast.

I don't understand why my other Facebook friends call orgies "housewarming" much like I don't understand why there are no tops left in Astoria. I don't wanna waste time traveling to White Plains! I wanna waste time getting wasted and spit roasted.

## MARCH 17

*Dear Diary:*

Hooked up with a guy named Rupert today. After swallowing him, I realized his sperm was protein-rich. I know this because when I overeat protein, my tummy makes weird sounds: *goop, goop, goop, bloop, bloop, bloop, and schloop, schloop, schloop.*

Rupert said, "What's that loud and obnoxious sound coming out of your stomach? Did you eat someone loud and obnoxious, like a drag queen?"

"Yeah, right. The first thing a drag queen does in my stomach is she starts lip-syncing all that *gooping, blooping,* and *schlooping* sounds. You're crazy, Rupert! The first thing a drag queen would do is go and count how much I swallowed, then tell my friends all about it. Then she would get wasted from the free-floating alcohol in my blood from the last night's party."

He said, "So what's your point?"

I said, "My point, Rupert, is this: the sound is not coming from my stomach. It's Alexa playing Mozart."

Rupert didn't believe me. He said he went to Juilliard and knew everything there is to know about Wolfgang Amadeus Mozart. Rupert started blurring out facts: Mozart this, Mozart that, *Mitridate re di Ponto, Misa Brevis in G.*

I said, "Listen, bitch, if I wanna hear foreign sounds, I'll add fiber to my diet, and on top of my *gooping, blooping,* and *schlooping,* I'll have some *ooing, booing,* and *fooing.*"

He said, "So what's your point?"

I said, "I don't need to spend four years in a fancy gay school like Juilliard to learn boring facts about Wolfgangs. But about gangbangs? Count me in! Look, if I wanna get to know someone better, I'll just have sex with them."

"What should I do to become famous?" he asked, switching the spotlight from me.

"Sweetie," I said, as I sniffed some poppers, "if you wanna become famous, don't accumulate all that school debt. Trust me, I went to culinary school, so I know a thing or two about handling debt and meat. If you wanna become famous, do what everyone else in Hollywood does: sleep with the producer."

## MARCH 18

*Dear Diary:*

After chatting with a cute neighbor on Grindr, I invited him over. Since I'm gay and love opening presents, I opened his pants the second he walked in. His schlong, however, gave off a cheesy smell, and I'm not talking mozzarella or apple-smoked Vermont cheddar. It was real bleu. It was so cheesy I became gassy just by smelling it.

When I told Stilton, "You have to go home. Your penis reeks!"

He said, "Why? It's natural."

"So is growing armpit hair, but you don't see the Kardashians with bushy underarms, do you?"

I understand he's young, in college, and on winter break, but have some class! Getting lazy is natural, but having a smelly penis is not. If you wanna be natural, fine, go live in fucking nature! I heard Mowgli was also single.

Besides, I'm lactose-intolerant!

## MARCH 19

*Dear Diary:*

Told Bagwis about my cheesy-dick encounter last night, and he said I should blame the Europeans because they don't circumcise their men.

I said, "Excuse me, bitch! I'm from Europe."

Bagwis said, "You're not from Europe, ho. You're from Siberia, which is technically in Asia."

"My point is, Bagwis, I don't walk around town smelling like a deli counter at Food Bazaar International."

Speaking of Europe . . . I don't trust Europeans. Last time the French tried circumcising, they did it in the wrong place, and we lost Marie Antoinette.

Bagwis said, "Maybe Stilton didn't have time to shower."

I said, "Bullshit. Even homeless people improvise. Have you read the news this morning? A guy taking the R Train couldn't find a restroom, so he pissed on a woman's face—so don't tell me there aren't any options."

Bagwis said, "Yeah. You can't find a restroom anywhere in New York unless you buy something to eat. The guy must have been broke."

I said, "Exactly—and hungry. I get him because I'm always broke, too. Why couldn't Stilton be classy like him and improvise a shower of some sort?"

"Some people don't have access to showers."

I said, "Ted Bundy didn't go around crying and complaining that he didn't have anyone to kill. He just did it. People should learn from the pros."

Bagwis said, "What's your point?"

I said, "Take a shower before a hookup is my point!"

## MARCH 20

*Dear Diary:*

I played my guitar after work and finished writing a new song. I know I'm gay and my mouth is always open and *blah, blah, blah,* but I know why I hate hooking up. My friend Nikita said it's because I like strings attached, and it's true for all the instruments I played or blew: and it's the same with all the penises I blew and played with.

## MARCH 21

*Dear Diary:*

I realized why I'm super anxious and bitchy today (yes, more than usual): I feel shackled down by my debt and credit card bills, but also I need some change in my life.

I risk sounding like a mad gay man, but what if I take my songs and go traveling? I know, I know. I need to learn how to drive first and get a driver's license.

I imagined myself as a music star and the reflection in my mirror cringed. I would be a horrible music star. I would be late for my own shows, just like I'm late for work now.

Being late isn't my fault because I'm a real New Yorker. Have you ever taken the New York City subway? I heard from my friend Avraham that his friend Azriel Goldberg was fifty minutes late for his own funeral because he took the Z Train, which runs slower than the brain of a Playboy bunny.

Change is hard and scary—but I have to quit my job before I go crazy.

The only job I'll never quit? The blow job.

## MARCH 22

*Dear Diary:*

Made chicken tacos for dinner and invited my friend Jose to try them.

He said, "They taste just like my sugar daddy!"

I asked him, "Why do you say that? Does your sugar daddy taste like a chicken taco?"

Jose said, "Don't be stupid. He's ninety years old and his penis—just like your chicken—is very tender. Thanks for making me feel right at home!"

## MARCH 23

*Dear Diary:*

Work was slow, so instead I was real-estate browsing. Several plots went down in price at Queens Cemetery and I've been eyeing the plot next to Louis Armstrong. When I die we could entertain each other by doing what we know best: blowing. We'll have parties every day! No hangovers! Plus, I won't need to show up for work the next day. And most importantly: no STDs—so bareback forever!

## MARCH 24

*Dear Diary:*

I can't get over how cheap the cemetery plots are, so I started thinking more about my own funeral. I invited Bagwis for dinner and told him, "I want everything to be gay and over the top at my funeral. So over the top I wanna be buried on the other side of the hill.

"Don't wear black at my funeral. I wanna see some color, and it doesn't matter which one unless it's white. So don't wear white because it will be after Labor Day."

He said, "Why not a summer funeral?"

I said, "I'm doing a favor for *you*, you tacky bitch. If I die in June, I don't want your sweaty balls up in my face. This will be the most fabulous day of my life. I'll have so much fucking makeup that even *Vogue* will put me on the cover: Bottom of the Month."

He said, "What kind of coffin do you want?"

I said, "Coffins are so nineties and I'm claustrophobic. If I wanna lie down in a tight space, I'll just stay in my apartment in Astoria. Listen, I want jazz, class, and pizzazz, so I wanna be buried in a brown Crate & Barrel ottoman."

My friends and enemies alike will say, "That's so Jeremy! He had such good taste."

My ex will say, "The coffin goes well with his eye, doesn't it? His brown eye, that is."

American Express will say, "Good taste, sure, but why are *we* the ones paying for the funeral?"

## MARCH 25

*Dear Diary:*

I'm agitated because I was trying to purchase tequila to make frozen margaritas, but my Russian accent came out, and they thought I said vodka.

Ugh, first world problems: now I have to make martinis instead.

## MARCH 26

*Dear Diary:*

I told my coworker over lunch, "Hung, there's a theory about the Earth being hollow, like Lindsay Lohan's brain, and I believe it. The documentary about it was very convincing."

I'm trying to change my life, so maybe it's time to change my beliefs.

Hung said, "You believe the Earth is hollow? Don't be stupid."

I said, "Yeah, right. Like I can change who I am."

## MARCH 27

*Dear Diary:*

Kids, drunk people, and the elderly have more in common than meets the eye. They shit their pants, say what they want, and don't have any money.

I'm like a drunk old kid (old, because I'm thirty-one in gay years). Besides, I like to play Bingo, I cry like a baby, and I like puzzles. For instance, it puzzles me why the guy from the bar never texted me last week. Maybe I'm not handsome enough. I quickly texted my friend Rafael, a celebrity makeup artist: *"Make me look hot!"*

He replied: *"I can't do magic, bitch. But let me microblade your eyebrows. Microblading will make your huge head appear smaller, shaping your face. Also, grow some scruff. I'm tired of your babyface."*

## MARCH 28

*Dear Diary:*

My eyebrows look great! Microblading, I learned yesterday, is a semi-permanent eyebrow tattoo that will last for one year. Yesterday, my eyebrows looked fine, but today they are scabbing and look unnatural as if I used a Sharpie. Rafael said they would look natural in a week, but for now I'm upset that I resemble Bozo the Clown with his exaggerated arches.

To feel better, I remembered a fun fact from culinary school: when you're proofing yeast and the yeast reproduces, it becomes a giant Bukkake orgy because they're all having sex and then multiply in minutes. It made me happier and hornier, so right now I have no regrets spending twenty-one thousand dollars on culinary school or having microblading done!

## MARCH 29

*Dear Diary:*

I was harassed on the subway today. Someone slapped my firm, sexy butt hard without my consent. It was one of those big, juicy slaps I only dream about when having sex. That would be nice in the bedroom, but not in a crowded car at nine in the morning. My tight pants have no room for a growing penis.

I turned around to give that guy a dirty look and realized what hit me was an enormous tote bag. Not a hand, a tote bag. What a disappointment, Diary. This incident could've been the beginning of a very significant relationship or at least a hookup.

## MARCH 30

*Dear Diary:*

Today, one of my annoying friends posted on Facebook that happiness is contagious. What's his point? So is oral gonorrhea, but I don't go advertising my past all over the internet.

(Like with the rule of Vegas, what happens in my mouth stays in my mouth.)

Listen, if you wanna talk about something contagious at least make it interesting. Positive affirmations, pro-gun hoopla, and catchy slogans make me sick. For instance, I hate this one: "Guns don't kill people. People kill people."

Is that so, Captain Obvious? *People* kill people? Wow, fucking shocking.

That kind of logic is like calling a guy with no picture on Grindr "straight."

What kinds of slogans are next, red states? I know what kind: "Men don't rape women. Penises rape women."

That can only partially be true. Guns are always up and ready to shoot, but penises are unpredictable, and when it's cold they shrink. Have you ever seen a gun shrink?

I got into an argument about guns with my Republican coworker Hung.

He said, "We need guns to protect our families."

I said, "If you need to protect your family, you don't need a gun, Hung. You need to buy yourself condoms to stop multiplying your white supremacist genes."

## MARCH 31

*Dear Diary:*

I feel like a fucking squirrel today . . . because I want some nuts in my mouth!

Why do I have to spend an entire day at work? I mean, have you ever seen a squirrel working? Me neither! Listen, when I'm horny I'm unproductive, and instead of "sick leave" gay men should have "horny leave."

How does it work? When you tell your boss, "I'm feeling horny and need to hook up," your boss says, "Okie dokie, get some pokie."

# APRIL

My new fish Kiki in her makeshift fish bowl, a Patron bottle.

## APRIL 1

*Dear Diary:*

Happy April Fool's Day! I've just downloaded Twitter. Just kidding—I've deleted it. I hate Twitter! You need to follow people and hashtag things.

When I tried following someone (a guy who lives across the street), I got a restraining order and can't follow him anymore. Just kidding again! I can still follow him. As long as nobody knows.

Turns out, after microblading, my eyebrows look fabulous, while scruff made my cheeks more defined, so little by little my face is changing.

Last year, a sadist dentist pulled my wisdom teeth out, and that procedure had people believe I'd lost thirty pounds.

With my weight going down I'll soon resemble a composite for Madeline McCann's kidnapper. Do you know what I mean? I recently watched a documentary about Madeline McCann's disappearance and the sketch artist had drawn an oval with hair—no eyes, nose, or mouth.

First of all, that's so homophobic. Where would a guy stick his penis if there's no mouth? And, second of all, my face finally looks oval—*oval*, not round!

## APRIL 2

*Dear Diary:*

I like how these drama queens complain about photoshopped pictures on the internet, but they never say a word about songs. Do they think, what, that it takes one take, and no autotune?

Every song is a combination of one hundred takes, thirty hours of instrument arrangements, and five blow jobs to the producer. How's that for reality? People will photoshop, airbrush, and blow as long as they are young and can keep their mouths shaped like an O.

If you want reality then stay at home. In the meantime, I don't care that Kourtney has six toes on her latest Instagram photo. Leave my Kardashians alone!

## APRIL 3

*Dear Diary:*

Had dinner with Bagwis, and it was outstanding—the dinner, not Bagwis. We went to a Korean restaurant on Broadway and Thirty-second Street.

We talked about diets, and Bagwis thinks that a sugar daddy should be called a Splenda daddy on keto diet, and I agree. If a daddy is into raw food, he should be called a bareback daddy.

Bagwis asked, "What if a daddy is into juicing?"

I said, "We will call him a juicy daddy."

Bagwis said, "And if he's vegan, what? We'll call him Carrot Top?"

In Alabama, where they don't know what a vegetable is, when they watched Carrot Top in *Sharknado 4*, they called him "Two Piece and a Biscuit."

## APRIL 4

*Dear Diary:*

Just finished reading a health article online, suggesting we should drink pickle juice for hydration. That's so dumb and ridiculous.

You could drink pickle juice or take a teaspoon of salt with water.

The thing is, salt with water is unprofitable and the pickle juice marketers pimp out the juice to make us spend our hard-earned bucks. The idea behind marketing pickle juice is beyond stupid. With similar logic, you could say, "She's not a sequoia, she's Kendall Jenner." Or "I don't suck dick, I'm Taylor Lautner."

The marketers will tell you similar lies, "Salt is unhealthy and can cause water retention, but this is not salt; it's pickle juice with minerals."

Diamond is a fucking mineral, bitch. Salt is for Salt Bae.

## APRIL 5

*Dear Diary:*

I'm now a proud father of a sapphire-colored betta fish! It's not beta, alpha, or gamma, or anything Greek and uncircumcised. It's *betta*. I wanted to name her Bitch because she looked like one, then I noticed she kept opening and closing her mouth more than me on Saturday night on my knees—as if she was having a kiki with Daddy! So I named her Kiki.

Gay men love their kiki. Just the other day, I was having a kiki with my best friend Bagwis. We discussed the United Nations and how there's this row of flags right in front of it. I know I'm Russian, but I can never tell apart the Russian flag from the French flag, Irish from Indian, or North Korean from communism.

My favorite must be the Turkish flag: a moon with a star. I'm all about astronomy and celebrities.

And did you see the Polish flag? The Polish were so lazy that they took a white canvas piece, started painting it red, finished half of it, and called it a day. In fact, the Polish wanted to name their country Pol-and-Pierogi-and-Vodka, but they got drunk on Belvedere and settled on Pol-and. When hangover hit, they dropped the hyphen.

Monaco was another lazy country. They stole the Polish flag and turned it upside down.

**APRIL 6**

*Dear Diary:*

I called out sick today. Everything is fine—I just hate my job. Plus, I must spend some quality time with Kiki today. We need to get acquainted, have a mimosa for brunch, and bitch about our lives.

To be productive, I emailed my boss, *"Let's discuss my raise."*

He emailed back, *"Why do you think you deserve one? You haven't lost any weight, you're always late, and today you didn't even show up!"*

In my email, I explained to him—my juicy butt, tardiness, and callouts aside—that I'd received over sixty thousand work emails over the past ten years. That's a lot of work!

I finished my email with: *"My lights are off and the door is ajar. I'll wear a blindfold when you come over. Condoms and lube are on the table."* Thank God I sent it on Grindr. That's the problem with multitasking and having two apps open simultaneously on my phone. Three times already I'd mistakenly emailed my address to my boss intended to my hookups, and once I accidentally sent my expense report to a hookup.

Somehow, if you divide sixty thousand emails by the number of days I worked, it ended up 17.97 emails per day.

How is it not an even number? I don't understand math or why people leave dishes in the sink without washing them. What happened to the last 0.03 of my emails? It's not like I'm lazy and couldn't finish them. Trust me, if there's anything I know how to do is how to finish everythi

Listen, I've just finished a whole apple pie in one seating for breakfast, so I know how to work. Ask the local hooker, Tanisha. My work ethic makes her look like she's on unemployment. Ask anyone I've ever gone down on! I suck so much that I'm afraid Astoria has become a fire hazard as I've sucked everyone dry.

Besides, I've received sixty thousand emails in ten years. Do you know how much postage that is? At fifty-five cents per letter, that's thirty-three thousand dollars. Not finishing the remaining point three percent is saving my boss forty-nine ninety. I know it's not a lot, but since I'm saving money it's something, OK?

It's noon, and I'm on my third martini, waiting for his reply.

My boss emailed back at one: *"You'll receive your raise when the sun turns blue or when you lose fifty pounds. Plus, wear* black on Thursday for the investor meeting. Black is slimming, and we all know you need that."

## APRIL 7

*Dear Diary:*

After a drunken night in the neighborhood, my friend Naan (yes, like the bread) said he wanted some Asian. I've been craving Peking duck for a while, so I suggested this great place in Astoria called Food Bazaar International. Their buffet is to die for. When we got there the store was closed, which makes sense as it was two in the morning.

We didn't give up, though, and went to drink at a local hole in the wall that's literally called Hole in the Wall. Naan and I didn't have any Peking, but at the bar I met this cute Asian guy—Jiang—and we went home for some poking.

Listen, if I want Asian, I get it.

## APRIL 8

*Dear Diary:*

I love facials, peels, and exfoliations. I have more facials in a week than I catch STDs. Last night, when Jiang from the bar said, "I wanna give you a facial," I got so fucking excited! I told him where I keep my facial tools, lay down, and enjoyed.

**APRIL 9**

*Dear Diary:*

An expensive painting for the office, which we'd ordered two months ago, arrived today: the painting depicts balls of different sizes against a white background and it's massive.

I emailed the artist to thank him: *"I love your balls—so nice and clean."*

He said, *"Did you get it in OK?"*
I said, *"It was hard."*
*"Is it hung? Send me a picture."*
*"It's hung."*
*"Is it too big?"*
*"It fits well and covered a big hole."*

Then I texted Bagwis and we had the same conversation about my hookup from yesterday.

Sex is just like art, but cheaper.


**APRIL 10**

*Dear Diary:*

Felt a little itchy in my peachy and went to get STD-tested. Last year, while busy with culinary school, I barely had sex (maybe five times a week maximum). I got hooked on coming to the free clinic because I knew I'd get touched for sure.

The rapid test results came back negative, but other results will take ten days. The doctor asked me if I had any questions and I had lots. I said I'd been gassy lately and wondered whether that was contagious or whether I could have gotten it from a blow job I'd given the night before. The guy I sucked off didn't look beefy but more fibrous, and I heard fiber makes you gassy.

The doctor calmly said, "You can't get gassy from a blow job. Just stay off greasy Paula Deen's recipes."

## APRIL 11

*Dear Diary:*

I don't understand our fascination with gruesome murderers. I'm watching Netflix, and every documentary is about a serial killer who murdered someone and then ate them, as if they were meat.

I should know a thing or two about meat: I'm a gay man, and I graduated from culinary school.

For me, presentation is everything and slicing someone in half just doesn't look appetizing—that's just a magic trick. Come on, Anthony Morley, have some class and put a little garnish on the plate. A rib of celery goes a long way. If you're in a pickle and don't have any garnish go to Central Park and pluck some flowers, or at least apply an Instagram filter.

Or just be creative! Ted Bundy once arranged his victims' vaginas in a concentric circle and served them with a homemade cocktail sauce, which went splendidly with seafood.

H. H. Holmes started following me on Instagram for my recipes and garnish ideas, so I told him, "Holmes, do what Jeffrey Dahmer does: add some color.

"I once went to Albert Fish's dinner party and while his ladyfingers were to die for, everything was red, red, red. Red doesn't go well with my skinny jeans. Boring! If I wanna eat red, I'll just eat rosacea off my cheek.

"And don't go for the obvious, Holmes, as serving sausages, giblets, and liver pâtés is so eighties. You need pizzazz. Order a clown! Ronald McDonald made billions of dollars by being one. Ronald also knows that variety is key. He serves burgers with beef, chicken, and sometimes Lindsay Lohan when she gains a little weight.

"You can also hire a hooker, Holmes. They know more about meat than a butcher.

"And last: it's all about texture. Try grinding the meat with some onions. If you don't know how to grind, go to the local fetish bar, Sub Way, and join the dance floor or a back room on a Saturday night."

## APRIL 12

*Dear Diary:*

I'm still on serial killers. I realized that it's not the manslaughters that I loathe, and I even barely mind cannibalism. Why judge anyone? Psycho Betty was a picky eater. So. Leave. Her. And. Other. Cannibals. (And. Britney.) Alone!

What I detest is when the killer has sex with the corpse. So rude and narcissistic. Joachim Kroll didn't care about whether his corpses enjoyed the sex part, and obviously the slaughter part was barely enjoyable. I mean, who likes to be stabled with a cold weapon? Warm it up in a microwave, bitch!

And his corpses were so quiet, too. What's fun about that? I like dirty talk during sex, so a corpse's no good to me. What's the dirtiest thing Kroll has ever heard? While working as a toilet attendant for Mannesmann, Kroll heard Hitler farting in a stall from his favorite liver dumplings.

## APRIL 13

*Dear Diary:*

Everyone is suing everyone these days. You haven't seen so many suits since the last Goldman Sachs board meeting.

Allen Heckard sued Michael Jordan, claiming Jordan looked like him. That "ruined" Allen's "career"—as Kanye West's chauffeur's assistant's drug dealer—and caused him "emotional pain and suffering." Why did he complain? I think it's cool to resemble a celebrity, even if you resemble Joe Exotic. I even have a dildo shaped like Henry Cavill's fist, and you have no idea how much pleasure it gives me!

Stacey Pincus sued Starbucks, claiming the coffee chain uses too much ice in their drinks. Bitch, it's called *iced coffee* for a reason. Aside from that, Starbucks was the best she could do?

Cleanthi Peters sued Universal Studios for its horror-themed attraction, saying she was too scared. Why was she scared? If you want something to be scared about, attend a white supremacist rally.

## APRIL 14

*Dear Diary:*

I keep thinking about all the lawsuits. I hate to sound like an old fart, but you didn't have to be meticulous when writing directions and instructions for your products before consumerism, but now? There are warnings on everything!

When the movie is rated PG-13, that's condescending to teenagers because everyone matures differently. Mentally, Lindsay Lohan is nine but she's allowed to sniff cocaine, speak with a

Greek accent, and watch porn. On the other hand, Prince William—at forty—still lives with his daddy and I'm jealous. I'd give anything to live with my daddy.

A sugar daddy, that is...

And by give anything, I of course mean give head.

Anyhow. Do we need directions on a box of toothpaste, for example? Is that because we accidentally may brush our teeth with a pussy the way Hugh Hefner does every morning?

I'm not talking about directions on medical products like painkillers, Gas-X, or black fisting gloves. I'm talking about instructions on grocery bags. True story! I was at Whole Foods the other day and saw "Hold both handles" printed on the paper bag.

To vent, I called Bagwis and sarcastically said, "Wait, I have to hold *both* handles? Good to know! Giving such unsolicited advice is beyond rude."

Bagwis said, "Why are you so cranky? Here's how I stay calm—"

I interrupted, "I'm cranky because I hate stupid recommendations. I'd never walk up to a pilot and say: 'Emilia, after you take off, don't forget to land,' much like I'd never tell my boss, 'Good morning, asshole. Instead of eating a carrot for lunch—insert it in your butt.'"

Bagwis said, "Here's how I stay calm when I'm angry—"

I interrupted, "When you get a package from Amazon, they even print in block letters whether the package is heavy—like I can't tell by lifting it. In the good old days when a package arrived, we didn't ask any questions. We opened the package and sucked it."

Bagwis said, "So to stay calm—"

I hung up.

I said no advice!!!

## APRIL 15

*Dear Diary:*

Today is Tax Day! I did mine so long ago that George Washington was still the president. I don't understand why people wait until the last minute to do their taxes and then wait in a curved line around a local post office trying to get "April 15" stamped on their returns. That's not patriotic. If you wanna stand somewhere where it's curvy, don't stand in line: stand in Richard Gere's pubes.

Also, why did it take them four months to find the post office? Fucking Columbus discovered America faster and even gifted blankets laced with chickenpox to the Native Americans. Columbus found the blankets along thrift stores in Red Hook, Brooklyn where the hipsters lived. Queens is different. When I shop at a local store in Astoria for some jeans they don't even have my size—28—let alone thousands of blankets last minute.


## APRIL 16

*Dear Diary:*

I've been thinking all day: how do you lace thousands of blankets with chickenpox? Wouldn't it be easier to lace them with poppers? Once the orgy starts, you learn who's the top and who's the bottom. Not that it's helpful to Columbus, but it's helpful at the Black Party—and in my bedroom.

But seriously, though, how did lacing blankets with chickenpox help the U.S. economy? Columbus spent thirty bucks at the store called Used Mama's, but where's the income and how did the taxpayers even benefit?

For instance, a good Republican Melania made her favorite lasagna with Cheetos for one thousand people. She spent a million dollars on the ingredients alone. Now *that's* patriotic!

## APRIL 17

*Dear Diary:*

I woke up hungover and feel like an everything bagel. There are black spots all over the place and my hole is tight.

I hate waking up at the crack of dawn but needed to squeeze in a run this morning because my stomach won't get flat by itself.

Lately, I spend more time on my feet than I spend on my knees, which seems highly unlikely. But since I'm a gay man, I wanna be controversial.

## APRIL 18

*Dear Diary:*

I've composed twenty-five songs in the past twenty days and I feel productive! I haven't felt this hot since the last sun flare.

Unfortunately, when I recorded myself sing I realized Hollywood won't be calling me. In fact, my landlady called me instead and said that if I wanted to keep that, quote, "loud, obnoxious, and annoying Pekingese," I needed to put down a five-hundred-dollar deposit first.

## APRIL 19

*Dear Diary:*

Today is Good Friday. After work, I went bowling with my best friend Bagwis. I'm gay so I love bowling or anything where balls are concerned.

After bowling we went to a steak house in Hell's Kitchen. I'm gay so I love my beef.

At night, Bagwis and I went to a Spanish gay bar, Dos Suckundos, and guess what? I'm gay so I love it when balls and beef are together in the same building.

So like I said: a really good Friday!


## APRIL 20

*Dear Diary:*

Came home from another run. I love running as much as Paris Hilton loves leaning over the toilet bowl with two fingers in her mouth. In fact, I've always thought I was born in the forest and that my mom's real name was Bunny.

My obsession with running started when I was six years old and had two giant front teeth with a gap in the middle. I looked like a rabbit. The gap was so massive I had to floss with a plunger.

At nine I was a rabbit for Halloween, and at twelve I started bar-hopping (it was Russia, so that's allowed). At fifteen I only ate carrots and watched movies with Carrot Top, and at twenty my ears grew longer, so at twenty-two, I picked up running.

That's evolution, bitch—look it up.

## APRIL 21

*Dear Diary:*

Today is Easter. In California they call it Wester, and in the North-East, it's a Nor'easter.

Speaking of Easter... I don't understand the connection between the Easter Bunny and Jesus, much like I don't understand the connection between Santa Claus and his multiple reindeer, or the Pilgrims and the turkey. I'm sensing bestiality a bit, which is fine only if your hookup is horse-hung and you're doing it doggy style.

Why couldn't Jesus, Santa, or the Pilgrims have sex with humans?

Last year, I barely hooked up because guys on Grindr blocked me after seeing my pictures. I was desperate for sex, but not once did I attend a farm to give head to a sheep. Instead, I went to Sheepshead Bay to a gay bar. (And if you wanna have sex with an animal that bar, Sweet Cheeks, is full of beasts.)

Anyhow, I only enjoy bunnies, reindeer, or turkeys if there's savory sauce on the side.

## APRIL 22

*Dear Diary:*

According to an ancient legend, when people from your past appear in your dreams, it means they've come to say goodbye and that you'll soon die. (Rumor has it, you die once every one of them says goodbye to you.)

In the past few months, people from my childhood and recent encounters appear in my dreams. I'm scared I'll die soon because there were maybe four hundred people I've met in my lifetime. One person a day comes to a year and two months to live!

I hope the legend includes hookups because then I could live for another ten to twenty years, or if it includes the ones I don't remember, maybe fifty.

## APRIL 23

*Dear Diary:*

Planet Mars got its own Kim Kardashian. In my opinion, NASA's Curiosity rover takes way too many selfies and seems a little needy.

I love space news and can listen for hours about planets and supermassive black holes, where gravity sucks so hard even light can't escape. That's fascinating! I wanna learn the black hole's technique and suck the lights out of someone. Perhaps I already have—but I don't suck and tell. My raw knees speak for themselves.

Curiosity is quite curious, by the way, maybe even a little *bi-*curious. I mean, how many rovers has NASA abandoned on Mars already? Don't you think that when Curiosity gets horny he seeks a quickie with Spirit or Opportunity in a dark alley?

I've seen all the available documentaries about Mars and I'll tell you one thing: if you wanna live in a land far away where it's lonely, freezing, and, most notably, *red*, don't waste five years traveling in a space shuttle.

Just go to Montana.

## APRIL 24

*Dear Diary:*

I'm sick and tired of hooking up and ready for a serious relationship. Even a date would do. I'm so desperate for a deep conversation I've been multitasking between five dating apps. Strangely enough, it's the same pool of people everywhere, and, like the twenty losers we are, we keep messaging each other on different apps expecting a different result.

It appears that everyone is coupled up except for me, Taylor Swift, and Adele. Even Flo from Progressive found a steady dick—I mean, a steady *gig*—and the gecko from Geico is fucking the duck from Aflac.

But there are no ducks for me, only horny boys on Grindr. So what's a boy to do? I cried for an hour, finished a martini, and popped an oxy, a cocktail that inevitably led to a threesome.

I'm not disappointed though, because lifting legs lifts my spirits!

## APRIL 25

*Dear Diary:*

I'm writing often about how horny I am and, for a change of pace, I wanna talk about my feelings.

Just kidding, bitch—it's still April Fool's month!

I wanna talk about my asshole—my asshole friend Oliver.

He's that friend who complains about his weight but refuses to have a salad or barf after eating a burger. I'm not body-shaming Oliver—bitch do whatever you like—but don't complain to me if you're unwilling to do the work. You can't have it both ways.

Oliver works from home—on unemployment—so his favorite activity is Netflix and chill on the couch. He's such a lazy bottom, too: he never travels for a hookup, climbs on top, or likes to be tied up to preserve energy.

The bitch has plenty of options to lose weight: liposuction, fat freezing, or even a haircut. Yes—anything that's on your body weighs you down. Why do you think I'm so meticulous about my trimming? Fuck the aesthetic; I wanna weigh less. Oliver could also try fasting, eating less fiber (it makes you gassy, and gas weighs a ton!), or drinking more water to flush out extra sodium.

"What do you think about all that?" I asked him.

Oliver said, "Nah. I don't care about my weight. I'm gay and my life is fabulous! I just wanna bitch about *something*."

## APRIL 26

*Dear Diary:*

My former roommate Nikita is in town from Boston for two days, so I won't have time to write. She and I lived together in Astoria years ago and stayed friends because we have lots of dirt on each other. When you share a wall and have big ears, you get to know a roommate well. I regret not installing a camera in her bedroom because I was despondent when she moved away from New York, and intense blackmail could've kept her around.

Sometimes I wonder why some people have so much impact on your life. Maybe Nikita is a witch. But, for now, welcome to New York, bitch!

## APRIL 27

*Dear Diary:*

Day-drank in Chelsea with Nikita, her boyfriend Juanito, and their four friends I'd never met before. The restaurant was on a boat—shaky and unstable like Nikita's sexuality. Another plus: when you wanna use the restroom, you pee straight into the Hudson River.

I was plastered and don't remember anyone's name, only the names I'd made up based on their physical appearance. The girl with whooping cough was Whoopi, the guy with weird jokes was Goofy, the girl with big boobs, red lipstick, and a tight skirt was Whore, her boyfriend—a hot beefy dude—Thor. I briefly wondered if Thor was planning on hammering Whore tonight, but I wanted to volunteer if she was not in the mood. I didn't say it out loud because I'm not Katniss Everdeen. Sometimes, things are better left unsaid.

Some straight guys believe that gay men are interested in them, but they're wrong—we're not interested, per se, we're just horny all the time, and that's two different things: like being a top and being discreet.

After five martinis, I couldn't spell "cat" let alone "Mississippi." Somehow though, I returned to Astoria, went out to a seedy gay bar called Double Penetration, and picked up a boy. We were both wasted and only managed to make out and dry-hump.

I was feeling great anyway, which is the real power of day-drinking and dry-humping.

## APRIL 28

*Dear Diary:*

I'm so hungover that I'll never drink again.

(Gotcha! It's still April Fool's month.)

Anyhow, I already went to a drag brunch and had five mimosas.

Drag brunches are ridiculously fun, especially if the drag queens have fun names like Penetration Exclamation or Gettys Burger.

I'm so old. I remember my very first drag brunch when I was twenty-four (back in 1841). I went with my friend Abraham Lincoln. At first, Abraham was confused about why we had to tip the drag queens or why nobody paid taxes on that money.

The queens Freeda Slaves and Keeptem Free put on a fantastic show, and Abraham loved it after getting wasted. He then confessed what really happened during his wrestling match with "The Glary's Grove Boys," which happened after his first glory hole boys.

Abraham said people were wild back in his day, and I know what he means. I was in politics myself and became famous in 1876 for proposing Amendment 28 after getting inspired by all the free libraries. But what about free hygiene?

So I proposed: "To yous, dirty bitches, I'll open free bathhouses, for I'm tired of sucketh a cheesy dick."

As you know, the amendment had never been passed by the House, but that evening I passed by a *bath* house, and the rest is history.

**APRIL 29**

*Dear Diary:*

Keep reminiscing. It's as if yesterday me and my pals wrote the Declaration of Independence. The one friend I miss the most is Thomas Jefferson—or as he called himself—TJ: he gave the best BJ.

I remember how back in the day we didn't call people in drag *queens*. We called them the House of Representatives. The House was led by George Washington, whose drag name was the Original RuPaul. There were more wig changes in those days than complaints about tuberculosis.

The most disappointing queen was Martin Van Buren. Why? He had access to coke and hookers—he was the president, after all—and you know what he chose? To look like Bozo the Clown. No wonder they called him Martin Van Ruins.

Fix your weave! The world is watching.


**APRIL 30**

*Dear Diary:*

I'm reading a history book and finished a chapter about the Declaration of Independence. The facts about it are incorrect! For instance, it says that Congress ordered the draft to "lie on the table." That's not how it happened. In reality, someone hacked into Thomas Jefferson's phone, and "lie on the table" had been his dirty text to me.

I was promiscuous back then, in my twenties. My favorite fuckboy was Franklin Pierce and he was fierce. The best cum guzzler of all the land . . . My chief complaint about the good old times is that people weren't having enough sex with each other and were dying from ridiculous diseases, like straining their eyes after bingeing on the Kardashians.

Everyone knows that to strengthen your immune system, you must exchange your microbiome with as many people as possible.

Why do you think gay men are so healthy? It's not because we follow fad diets or because we exercise regularly.

We *fuck* to live longer.

# MAY

Down to 145 pounds after working out and douching!

## MAY 1

*Dear Diary:*

My life is *totally over!* No, I'm not being dramatic, I'm not overreacting to gaining a pound, and no, I didn't go to a spin class.

I'm losing my hair! Have you any idea what getting bald means for a millennial? When a young gay man starts losing his hair, it means a disaster. To put this into perspective, it's akin to a lesbian losing a screwdriver or Mama June losing her meth.

Last year, I tried all sorts of shampoos, exfoliators, and thickening products. Like a loser, I also tried washing my hair with eggs, mustard, and beer. Nothing worked.

After some research, I learned that balding happens during testosterone breakdown when it releases a DHT compound that comes through sweat and damages hair follicles. There's medication—finasteride—that helps block that compound from the inside, and you have to shampoo every day to wash off whatever DHT seeped through. Finasteride is my last chance to have hair so I ordered it. I crossed my fingers and crossed my legs. When a guy came over for a hookup, I dutifully uncrossed my legs.

I'm getting a girl roommate in two days to help me pay the bills. Her name is Anna and she lives in Louisiana with her family, but we met in New Jersey years ago when Anna went to undergrad in Bloomfield College (or Shithole, as it's colloquially known). Anna was taking part in a hotdog eating contest, and when she swallowed fifty wieners under a minute, we became good friends. Someone with so much technique, I thought at the time, could teach me a thing or two about swallowing wieners.

The tea is this: Anna wants to live in New York to jumpstart her panty-designing career, and I need a roommate to help me pay the bills. As a present, I bought Anna a mattress from Amazon, but since my apartment has recently been exterminated, I told her to bring her own bedbugs.

(Look, I don't mind sharing but I'm not feeling generous at the moment. I figure, offering my place to someone who's never lived on her own is generous enough and anything extra is overkill.)

Anna is slightly prudish so I cleaned my entire apartment. I also hid any dildo I could find and voila! My place is roommate-ready. I'll miss my favorite dildo with a suction cup at the end that I keep in the shower, but these are the absurd things I do just to have some cash coming in. Disgusting! Am I even a gay man anymore?

**MAY 2**

*Dear Diary:*

After smoking some weed called Gorilla Glue #4, I received a bizarre massage from Jessica. She turned me around and started massaging Truth, my penis.

"Is this OK?" she asked.

Was Jessica crazy? OK? It was most certainly *not* OK! A woman hadn't touched my shlong in so long that when Jessica put her stinky hands on him, Truth crawled inside me to hide. He kept crawling and crawling until he fell out of my mouth, jumped in my shoes, and hopped away like a weird-looking, uncircumcised bunny on a slope.

When I finally caught up to him, the shlong said, "Listen, ho, we need to talk. I know you enjoy massages because you like getting poked. But why can't you be like me? Get a pedicure or Prince Albert, for example! But if you let Jessica—or any other woman—touch me one more time, there's no amount of Viagra that can save me. I'll retire so far away in Hawaii that the only eruption you'll ever experience is through a fucking volcano."

I thought Truth was overreacting.

I said in a baby voice, "I'm sorry, Truth. I'll speak to Jessica, and she'll never touch you or your two furry friends again. Plus I'll give you a nice rub later this evening, OK? Just get indoors already—it's fucking raining outside!"

## MAY 3

*Dear Diary:*

Today, my friend Anna arrived from Louisiana, if that's how you spell that selfish state. Yes, they're selfish in Louisiana because their obesity rate ranks them #1 in the country, and North America is tilting toward them. I don't mind slides but sometimes I wake up in New Jersey. Plus, all that fried chicken Louisianans eat damages—no, not the arteries—our livelihoods. The other day, I tried to order a down pillow and a harness but nothing with feathers or leather is even available anymore! Disgusting!

Anyhow, I picked up Anna at the train station at five.

That's right: She. Fucking. Took. A. *Train.* From. Louisiana. Yes. She. Did.

She was on the train for two days and smelled like Mick Jagger after a concert.

My first question was: "Bitch, the train? Serious?"

She said, "The train is cheaper than flying."

I saw smoke coming from her lying pants because they were on fire. There's nothing wrong with saying you're scared of airplanes. Even Peter Pan took a Xanax before flying to Alabama. Or was it Neverland? I can never remember as neither residents refuse to grow up or become Democrats.

But the *Boeing 737* is way safer and more entertaining than the *Orient Express*. When you take the *Boeing*, for example, you feel like you're jumping on a trampoline. You just go *Boeing, Boeing, Boeing*. And then a gay flight attendant brings you free juice, peanuts, and a hand job—or is it just me?—and you're in New York under two hours.

Do you know what you'll get on the train? Scoliosis.

My L5 and T9 are out of whack because of the fucking subway!

## MAY 4

*Dear Diary:*

Today on May 4, 1865, Abraham Lincoln was buried in his hometown, Springfield. John Wilkes Booth actually shot him on April 14 in Washington, but it took three weeks to get Lincoln delivered to Illinois. They must have used USPS Ground.

When I die, please treat me like Lincoln and bury me in my hometown in Siberia using the guidelines I outlined on March 24. You don't even need an ice pack to conserve my corpse because Siberia is basically a freezer. However, choose two-day shipping because I don't want to spend three weeks in transit.

Anyhow, there's a massive hole in Anna's jeans near the crotch. I swear, her pussy came out and meowed a few times, scaring my fish Kiki. Is Anna from Louisiana or a dumpster on Battery Avenue in Dyker Heights? I don't need sloppy friends because they make me look overweight.

Anna says she's broke and can't afford new clothes, but what kind of an excuse is that? I'm broke too, bitch! But because I'm classy I never show my holes until it's dark out and the lights are dimmed.

## MAY 5

*Dear Diary:*

Today is Cinco de Mayo (or the Fifth of May in Spanish). I invited Anna to a local Mexican restaurant. I wanna learn Spanish this year so when I order my food I could say in Spanish, "Guacamole, margarita, burritos." But every time I'm at a Mexican restaurant they speak English to me, and I never get a chance to practice.

It took Anna three hours to get ready, which was annoying, but when we finally left I realized Anna failed to bring an umbrella.

I said, "It's raining, ho."

She said, "It's OK."

For a second I thought she was a goose and the water just splatters off her weave. But then while walking to the restaurant, Anna had the nerve to ease under my umbrella and say, "Is this OK?" She sounded like Jessica on Thursday!

I rolled my eyes but chose to say nothing. After all, Anna's been in New York for only three days, so if I must kill her I'll let her enjoy life and Mexican food for at least a week.

How come people from Louisiana can't seem to notice my space bubble, which is an exclusive club, resort, and spa? To get the membership and use my steam room, baths, and other facilities, you must have at least one of the following: look hot like Leonardo DiCaprio in *Titanic*; look mediocre like Leonardo DiCaprio in *The Great Gatsby*; or look ratchet, like Leonardo DiCaprio in *The Revenant*.

Did you get my point? Be male!

## MAY 6

*Dear Diary:*

Speaking of mail, Anna from Louisiana doesn't recycle the cardboard boxes she receives. But that's not even the worst. Today she used up an entire roll of toilet paper in one sitting. Does she have seven assholes she needs to wipe? I'm all about hygiene and I understand the difference in her anatomy, but toilet paper is expensive.

To avoid using toilet paper, my pedicurist Olga uses a portable bidet, which is a water bottle she squirts in her pussy. She saves trees, eliminates plastic, and quenches thirst with one device. Olga is quite a multitasker. If everyone were like Olga (her face aside), the world would be a better place.

I promise I don't pussy-shame Anna, but I told her three days ago, "Feel free to use as much paper as your holes want. But have the decency to cross the street toward the grocery store and steal two rolls from any restaurant next to it. There are dozens of them in Astoria."

## MAY 7

*Dear Diary:*

Received a lousy haircut in Elmhurst today. Why was I in Elmhurst in the first place? A hookup, naturally! While I was in the neighborhood I stopped at a barbershop. My hairstylist was from Paraguay, but when I mispronounced it as "Para*gay*" Ramon misunderstood and got offended.

He said, "I'm not gay!"

"Why are you so bitchy?" I asked. "It's not like I said you were from North Dakota."

Ramon misunderstood again, so now I look like Dakota Johnson.

## MAY 8

*Dear Diary:*

I woke up feeling like Palm Springs in June: gay, old, and with a temperature of a hundred and three. I went to the doctor who said it was the flu—not during the flu season, mind you, but in May. I probably got it yesterday from my hookup, my hairstylist Ramon, or Anna. I told the bitch to bring bedbugs from Louisiana, not the fucking flu.

It makes sense that I caught the flu offseason because I've always been a rebel, and since I'm gay, being controversial is vital. Examples: I've slept with a Republican at a Democratic convention; I don't match my outfits, because they match themselves; last, I drink my cold brew coffee hot and through a straw.

Since my temperature was over a hundred, I took advantage and saved on my electric bill. Instead of cooking on the stove, I cracked two eggs and fried them right on my chest without any oil!

My skin is oily enough.

## MAY 9

*Dear Diary:*

Anna from Louisiana came home yesterday and said, "I wanted to get you something for your flu, but didn't know what, so I didn't get it."

I said, "The flu doesn't need anything. The flu's fine!"

Anna said, "I also wanted to get you something to eat, but didn't know what, so I didn't get it."

You know what else she doesn't get? If she keeps bugging me while I have the flu, I'm going to a FedEx store and ship her back to Louisiana or Texas—whichever is fucking cheaper.

## MAY 10

*Dear Diary:*

Sick and tired of the flu. Sick because of the flu and tired because of Anna from Louisiana. She's clueless! Like today when she said, "I'm having meat for breakfast," I automatically assumed she'd invited a hipster over. No, by meat she meant bacon. She's from Louisiana, after all, so she loves her meat. I'd choose a hipster over bacon any day.

Anna heated a cast iron pan to high heat. When she added ten bacon slices, the bacon started burning and splattering all over the place. Listen, I went to culinary school, so I know a thing or two about burning and splattering. Smoky the Bear got fucking lost there today. The kitchen was so smoky and hot that I felt like I was in Cuba inside a cigar and that some uncircumcised communist was smoking me.

I understand that Anna is from Louisiana and likes it hot, but we need to establish what's hot before the summer starts.

Abs? Hot. A naked hipster in my bedroom? Super hot. But a burning apartment (or a burning itch on my crotch) is not. If you want to burn my apartment, fine, but first buy me some rental insurance (or an anti-itch cream).

**MAY 11**

*Dear Diary:*

Today is Saturday and I magically recovered from the flu. I always recover on weekends from any ailments because I hate my job. To drown my sorrows, I made some martinis—plural.

I got sozzled after three and sent dirty pictures of my banana to five guys. Ernie from Tennessee replied and he's coming over in ten minutes. He says he's deficient in potassium and needs my banana stat.

I wonder why people call Tennessee, *Tennessee*. That's a fucked-up name. Is it just me or are there more letters in Tennessee than people in that state?

Hold on, googling Tennessee.

Oh, wow: it says Aretha Franklin is from Tennessee. Is it just me or is Franklin a good name for a pasta sauce? I'm just hungry and craving pasta right now. Look, aside from shlongs, my mouth can always accommodate a starch.

Hold on, looking up the formula for starch.

It says: HO-HO-HO-OH-OH-OH. Is it a formula, is someone laughing, or did I just see three Ohios in a row?

Everyone's a ho this day, Diary. I'm tired of hooking up and want a serious relationship. I'm happy Bagwis wanted me to keep a diary. So when I have martinis, I'm honest with myself and have proof on paper that I want a partner.

Hold on, Tennessee Ernie just buzzed in.

Gotta go feed him some potassium.

## MAY 12

*Dear Diary:*

Today is Mother's Day, and since I don't have a mother in the United States, I wanna talk about Mother Teresa. Was she a mother, though? Because I don't remember her having any children.

Mother Teresa was born in the Ottoman Empire, an archaic name for Macedonia until Ingvar Kamprad invented IKEA and ottomans went out of style. Don't mix Macedonia with Macadamia—a nut. I've made that mistake once while having martinis and got a ticket to the capital, Skopje.

Mother Teresa's real name was Agnes Gonxha Bojaxhiu, which from the Ottoman language roughly translates to Matron "Mama" Morton. For legal rights, she had to go with what wasn't already taken and became Mother Tesla. Then Elon Musk sued her for everything she had (which was nothing), so she changed it to Mother Teresa.

In 1979, after receiving a Nobel Peace Prize, Mother Teresa refused to have a banquet thrown in her favor and asked to have the banquet money donated to India's poor. So unoriginal and stupid!

Look, everyone is sending money to the poor these days but that's not clever at all. If Mother Teresa had invested that money in marijuana stock, which cost pennies at the time, she could've fed the entire India, most contestants on *The Biggest Loser*, and some of Mama June.

What I love about Mother Teresa is that she was basically a gay man: she barely ate, traveled all over the world, and—because she was such a Virgo—she thought missionary was boring.

## MAY 13

*Dear Diary:*

I was thinking all day about the banquet Mother Teresa refused to have. Maybe she was smart because she had high blood pressure and needed to lay off saturated fat and salt. I decided to follow Mother Teresa's example and eat less salt this week, not only because I care about the children and *blah, blah, blah*, but because salt retains water and bloats your face. And I hate to look stocky. You simply can't call yourself a proper gay man when you give up on your appearance.

Do you know what else I hate about salt? The variety. Have you been to Food Bazaar International lately? They sell salt that's white, pink, and all fifty shades of grey. There's garlic salt, onion salt, and *salt* salt. Coarse grind, fine grind, and just Grindr. Kosher, Himalayan, Celtic Sea... It's so pretentious and fake!

Salt is salt.

But because I went to culinary school, people often ask me which salt is better. Just last week my chiropractor asked me, "Do you recommend *fleur de sel?*"

*Fleur de sel* sounds French and annoying.

I told him, "A-wut, you eat table salt at the table, sea salt with seafood, and flaky salt with your flaky friends. Serve Kosher salt to your Jewish friends, *fleur de sel* to your French friends, and when it comes to servicing yourself you have Grindr or your right hand."


## MAY 14

*Dear Diary:*

Salt is not the only product at Food Bazaar International that's fake. Did you know that tea—all of it—comes from the same plant: Camila Cabello?

Oh, wait, let me google.

*Camellia sinensis.*

I'm glad I refreshed my memory as I always mix up the two. Camellia sinensis produces tea leaves and Camila Cabello produces bad songs.

Tea is a scam! White, green, and black tea are made from the same plant. The longer tea leaves oxidize, the darker and more caffeinated tea becomes. White tea is picked, green tea is picked and fried, and black tea stains your teeth. So how do you turn a single plant into a multi-billion-dollar business?

You need smart marketing.

Meat companies know this too. They don't make money on pork alone and waste nothing from a pig—be it pigskin, prosciutto, or Kevin Bacon.

We live in 2019 and conventional beef is more boring than McClusky, North Dakota. To make a buck, meat companies must be crafty, so now we have lean, pasture-raised, and even vegan beef. So boring and unoriginal. Everybody knows we can find chuck, tenderloin, and brisket in one cow, but in Bear Gryll's mouth? We can find ants, worms, and crickets. You know where else you'll find crickets? At one of Sting's concerts. Look, if I wanna get stung, I'd rather visit Central Park and stick my head into a beehive.

Anyhow, tea is a scam!

**MAY 15**

*Dear Diary:*

I pulled a Mother Teresa today and didn't eat all day because I'm fasting. I consider fasting not so much as an eating disorder but more like passion.

Look, everyone is doing it: the Jews, the Muslims, and the supermodels. Vanity aside, there are tons of health benefits. Did you know that our cells are cannibals and when there's no food in the stomach the cells start eating themselves? The cells run after each other, swallowing everything in sight.

You can't even swallow semen while fasting because it has a hundred and fifty calories, so if you want the jizz, stay skinny by getting a facial.

**MAY 16**

*Dear Diary:*

After eating salt substitute all week (plus fasting, running, and taking diuretics to flush extra sodium out of my system), I'm finally skinny like a supermodel!

I messaged Tennessee Ernie: "Hey, do you wanna come over for round two of my Russian banana?"

He replied: "I guess."

You guess??? You do or you don't. There's nothing to guess!

Ernie was an utter disappointment today. I understand they're one hour behind in Tennessee, but did Ernie have to be behind on his sex skills too? He put his pants down, finished without even groaning, and left in four minutes flat.

From now on, the bitch can shop at Whole Foods for his banana needs!

I'm through with hookups—for real this time!

**MAY 17**

*Dear Diary:*

After an LGBT fundraiser, Bagwis and I visited a local gay bar in Astoria called Butt Plugs. A handsome guy at the bar was checking me out, so when I ordered a drink we started chatting. He said he was from Ecuador and introduced himself as Carlos. Plural. I was drunk and wondered if there were two of them, Carlo One and Carlo Two. Carlo One danced with me while Carlo Two bought me another drink.

I figured out Carlos was a vegetarian. How did I know? He was the only one not looking at me like a piece of meat.

After a while, we were dancing and kissing and then at midnight—no, he didn't turn into a pumpkin or was a figment of my imagination—we watched a drag show together; me holding his hand and him holding my ass. The more time we spent, the more I liked him.

How do I know I liked him? Well, I didn't go home with him, and I only go home with people I don't like.

I gave Carlos my phone number and invited him to a house party tomorrow night. I wanna get to know him. Not only because he's cute and has beautiful legs, but since he's from Ecuador he can teach me Spanish—hopefully for free.

**MAY 18**

*Dear Diary:*

I met Carlos at a gay bar in Hell's Kitchen called Boxers. It's either a spinoff from a lesbian bar called Bras or a spinoff from a Million Moms Against Ellen's bar called Losers.

Carlos is so unbelievably charming I can't stand it. After a couple of drinks, we walked to the house party hand-in-hand as if we were a couple. We were bonding fast and had enough chemistry in us to become hydrogen bonds.

After the party Carlos walked me to the subway on Forty-second Street, and we were making out for twenty minutes by the entrance. We were so annoyingly cute that even a homeless guy next to us finally stood up, pulled up his pants, and went across the street to continue taking his shit.

## MAY 19

*Dear Diary:*

I know it's only been three days but I'm already in love with Carlos! He sent me the cutest text this morning with a GIF of a Munchkin from *The Wizard of Oz*.

I'm totally a smitten kitten.

*The Wizard of Oz* has become a gay favorite, and why wouldn't it? Rainbows are all over the place, people are dancing, and there's also a poppy field, which I assume can only be slang for "parTy" drugs.

In the good old days when I was a twink, to find out if someone was gay, you asked them whether they were a friend of Dorothy. Now you just look on Grindr and you know whether they're gay or not. But how can you tell if someone's a queen?

Gay men are obsessed with the word "queen." We give each other labels such as a "drag queen," a "potato queen," or a "rice queen" (someone who exclusively sleeps with Asians).

There are also drama queens, size queens, and Queen Bee, who is really just Beyoncé.

As for me, I live in Astoria, so I guess I'm a queen from Queens.

I know I went through a thousand unrelated thoughts, but that's what Carlos's love does to my soul. Can you even imagine what it could do to my hole?

## MAY 20

*Dear Diary:*

Carlos called me today during lunch and slowly said that he had just got laid—

—off.

I was glad before yelling at him I heard the last "off." I was gonna shout, "You just got *laid* and you're calling me to brag, you asshole?"

Thank you, Virgin Mobile, for a clear, uninterrupted service.

Carlos sounded upset and I understand completely. I'd be upset too if I lost a job unexpectedly after working somewhere for five years. His company was undergoing restructuring and, therefore, downsizing, letting go other employees as well.

Carlos worked for an investment bank as a salesperson, which is why I believe we're a match—because I'm good at buying! A plus and a minus go together like a top and a bottom. As long as it's not too big, it just fits, you know?

Carlos felt terrible and embarrassed about being let go.

I told him, "A job is a job, whether you work for an investment bank, on Broadway, or getting a quickie in a dark alley. Jobs are always available and something will soon be open, like Stormy Daniels' mouth."

My pep talk slightly pacified him and I was impressed by how adult I sounded.

Does that mean I'm actually ready for a relationship?

## MAY 21

*Dear Diary:*

Carlos and I had our second date, a play on Broadway he had an extra ticket for. He was visibly depressed about getting laid off, but our date, he said, perked him up.

First, we had dinner at a Vietnamese restaurant in Hell's Kitchen where I showed Carlos my mad chopstick skills. Then, at the play, we held hands throughout the entire performance like a real couple.

I hadn't told Carlos about psoriasis on my balls, and since he held my right hand, I had to scratch my groin with my left. At least it was dark and nobody saw me. But since I'm not a leftie and bad at trigonometry, it was hard for me to reach the right angle. At some point I missed my crotch and by mistake scratched the balls of a daddy sitting next to me.

I leaned in and whispered, "I apologize. I don't know where my head is today."

The daddy winked and whispered, "No worries. I don't know where my head is either. Wanna be the first head of the day?"


## MAY 22

*Dear Diary:*

Anna from Louisiana is driving me crazy! She does her laundry in the kitchen sink together with the dishes, or what she calls multitasking. How's that multitasking? We don't live in 1786 where they had to wash dishes and clothes together because they had no choice.

I said, "Why are you acting like you're from a trashy state like Alabama or Alaska? You live in New York now. Learn the fucking manners."

"What manners?"

"Do your laundry at a Laundromat like a normal person!"

She said, "I don't have enough money."

I said, "You don't have ten dollars? Then how come when you're at Food Bazaar International you buy everything organic? Including extra firm cucumbers I've *never* seen you eat."

She said, "I buy organic because I care about my health."

"I care about my health too, which is why I don't want your dirty panties next to my IKEA dinner plates."

"Fine!" she yelled.

"Anna, if you lie, go big or go home. With the number of lies you tell I have a feeling you miss Louisiana and wanna go home."

"Maybe I do!"

"Then, *s'il vous plait*. It's French for 'please, be my guest.'"

## MAY 23

*Dear Diary:*

After confabulating with Anna, I've been thinking about the biggest lies and conspiracies. Not just Anna's ass big but *world* big. Since I'll watch just about anything as far as space is concerned, I watched a documentary about the flat Earth model.

That's fucking right: some people believe the Earth is flat, and there are already three hundred of them.

Not only do they believe the Earth is a piece of flatbread with walking chunks of meat, but they also genuinely believe an enormous light bulb—the sun—bakes us. It makes no sense! How would we plug it? Where will we find an outlet as big as Barbra Streisand's schnozzle?

"Flat-Earthers," as they're known, also explain how the shooter of John F. Kennedy disappeared: after he shot the president, the shooter was hiding near the end of the Earth and then swoosh! Accidentally fell down the hatch! But where is the end? Wouldn't we find it by now? I mean, the scientists took an *atom* apart, and if that accomplishment wasn't big enough, they took it down further into quarks. Quarks are ridiculously small, kind of like my paycheck.

One Flat-Earther said, "The end of the Earth is at the end! You have to be Stevie Wonder to miss it."

Something doesn't add up there, people! The only flat things around here are my stomach and Victoria Beckham's ass.

**MAY 24**

*Dear Diary:*

I watched more conspiracy theory documentaries. Some people speculate that Kim Kardashian staged her own robbery in Paris. Why on *flat* Earth would she steal from herself? The government already takes thirty percent of our income, and if we steal from ourselves, we won't have any money left to spend on slutty underwear. True, a jockstrap doesn't cover much, but I'm happy as long as it covers my junk.

Speaking of junk—can I vent about Adolf Hitler? Back in the day there was a conspiracy theory that Hitler had a double, and it was the double who killed himself in 1945, while Hitler moved to Argentina.

Look, Argentina is an excellent country, but Hitler was clearly not patriotic, nor was he a gay man. Did you see his outfits? None of them matched.

I'm so old that I was there in 1945 right before the Soviets captured Berlin.

I told Hitler, "Adolf, retire to Palm Springs or Key West. If you have less money, go to Kansas City, Kansas, or Tennessee—there's no income tax. Spend your money locally. Why are you going to fucking Argentina? Are you trying to blend in? People from Argentina are tan and gorgeous and they'll sniff you out with your ugly black mustache, that unflattering red swastika, and your vomit-green uniform."

I don't know where he went.

If Hitler tried to blend in, he probably went somewhere where it's black, red, and green. I hate stirring the pot and inspiring conspiracies, but have you seen the flag of Malawi?

## MAY 25

*Dear Diary:*

It's 3:30 in the morning and I'm reading a conspiracy book about the moon. I'm so excited I can't sleep a wink or, in the gay world, can't sleep a twink.

Some people truly believe we've never landed on the moon. Then where have we landed, Sherlock? We've all seen the footage: it was cold, isolated, and barren. Do you think we've landed in Crested Butte, Colorado?

It makes no sense why anyone would lie about going to the moon. If you're going to be embarrassed about going somewhere shitty, simply avoid Wyoming.

Listen, there's no need to hide your whereabouts, especially when the government tracks our every move. Thanks to the O.J. Simpson trial, we learned that cops can tell which tower your cellphone reception is coming from down to a mile. Creepy, right? Not as creepy as the suspect's name: O.J. What kind of a name is that? Did he work for Tropicana in Florida? Does he have any pulp? Can I add him to my vodka cocktail?

If I had a lazy eye and somehow missed the moon, my best friend Bagwis would tell everyone where I really went.

He'd say, "Jeremy was horny and went to Uranus and Neptune. Nobody replied on Grindr and he wanted to see two giant blue balls."

**MAY 26**

*Dear Diary:*

I overheard one of the investors talking about penetration at the office. Penetration this, penetration that. I was like, are we working or are we inside a steam room at my gym?

When I got home, I said, "Alexa, define 'penetration.'"

Alexa said, "Penetration is a successful selling of a product or service in a specific market."

An economic term—how boring!

Alexa is obviously not a gay man because "penetration" was Carlos and me last night! After waiting for seven days—a decade in the straight world—we finally had our first sleepover. Even

Bagwis was like, "Come again? A whole week? I can't wait for more than an hour."

But I'll say the following: quick hookups are fun to a point, but there is a way to successfully "sell your product or service in a specific marker" *without* penetration.

No, I'm not talking about oral sex.

I'm talking about love! I wanted a relationship for a long time, and Carlos may be the guy for me. The longer I wait before penetration happens, the longer our relationship will bloom like—

What are those flowers called again? I forget.

Oh.

Forget-me-nots.

The point is, the longer you wait, the longer your relationship will last.

When I like a man the way I like Carlos, my "lotus flower" turns into a prissy "touch-me-not," and my "rosebud" wants to wait before it's open for business.

I'm always so fucking poetic when I'm in love, talking about flowers and shit!

**MAY 27**

*Dear Diary:*

Today is Memorial Day, which means starting today, up until Labor Day, I'm wearing white every single day. That's why I hate the Pope: he never adheres to any gay rules and wears white even in the winter! So rude.

Memorial Day is for creating memories, so I visited Flushing to volunteer for people with Alzheimer's.

I hate that asshole Alzheimer and it's twofold. First, I must google how to spell his name—which is so selfish of him. He could've changed his last name to something simpler like Crohn, Tourette, or Parkinson—but, second, Alzheimer has a disease named after him and I'm gonna die unknown!

Life's not fair.

When I die, I want a disease named after me. When some guy (let's hypothetically say it's my coworker Hung) comes to work and tells everyone he's sick with Taylor's, my boss will ask him, "What's it like to be sick with Taylor's?"

Hung will say, "I'm gay, fabulous, and broke. I heard there is no cure."

**MAY 28**

*Dear Diary:*

I'm in love with Carlos. This morning at eleven he texted me just to say hi and wish me a good day. We text each other every minute so my phone is continuously discharged. I don't need any presents or be on top of the Eiffel Tower, I just need to be on top of *him*.

**MAY 29**

*Dear Diary:*

My coworker Hung told me today, "I like your sweater. You always know how to match your outfits. It's probably because you have the gay gene."

"Yeah," I said, "it's because I have the gay gene."

What I didn't say was: "Similar to you, Hung, who has the stupid gene. Listen, ho, being a gay man is a curse. I'm exhausted from drawing attention to myself and being on display like a queen. I'm tired of trying to lose weight, spending three hours getting ready for work, and jogging every day just to keep my juicy ass in check. So, anyway, Hung, how's your ugly nephew doing? He's very ugly, by the way. It's probably because you have the ugly gene too."

Some things are better left unsaid, especially at the office. But once I quit, expect a shitstorm!

**MAY 30**

*Dear Diary:*

Tonight is the finale of *RuPaul's Drag Race*, which is my favorite TV show. There's nothing like watching tall wigged men do death drops in heels. By the way, have you met Bob the Drag Queen—also known as Bob the Giraffe? He's twelve feet tall, which means I could never do drag at five foot eight.

When I was eleven, I remember wearing my mom's red heels around the house while she worked at the butchery chopping beef, but that was the extent of my drag career. I distinctly remember hiding my willy between my legs and looking in the mirror, thinking, "God has big plans for you, bitch!"

After *RuPaul*, Bagwis and I went to see a live drag show by Matt the Drag Queen and Sea Caucus, who performed at a local watering hole, Mary Poppers.

The owner Mary is a friend of mine and she's obsessed with gay men. I love having allies, and if ever we went to war, Mary is the one who'd save your life. She'd supply the alcohol, drag queens would supply the fabulousness, and I'd be on a gay cruise, but I'd be on the battleground in spirit.

## MAY 31

*Dear Diary:*

Carlos and I went out of the country today, to Brooklyn—yes, all the way across Manhattan Bridge. We attended a house party for a girlfriend of his and I like showing my tight ass to people I don't know.

At first I missed Astoria, but the party was in Crown Heights, which meant there were crowns. If there were crowns there were queens, and if there were queens I was almost home in Queens!

Carlos and I got wasted at the party, and I may or may not have been fingered in the cab home (I don't get fingered and tell).

What a month May has been! A cute guy is fingering me and my roommate is fucking with me. What can I say? I'm a true gay man and sex naturally comes to me.

# JUNE

In Montreal in my whore-shorts.

## JUNE 1

*Dear Diary:*

My friends (who are drag queens) invited me to their barbecue. I have to clarify they're drag queens because drag queens are amazing, FYI. People love mentioning celebrities because that moves them up the social ladder.

For instance, my Republican coworker Hung once said, "I know Melania and Donald Trump personally. Before they became the FLOTUS/POTUS, back in 2007 I knew them as Hocus/Pocus."

I asked Anna from Louisiana if she wanted to join the barbecue and Anna declined, saying she was busy doing laundry and needed to cook and clean. That, of course, meant she'd sit on her ass all day and do nothing. I hate that she combs her weave so often her hair is all over the fucking place. Sometimes I feel like I live with a Maltese puppy and from time to time, I bring her leftovers in a doggy bag.

Today, Anna's hair looked like she got caught in a magnetic field, all huge and puffy. I was scared the magnetic field would discharge my phone so I quickly skedaddled with a bottle of rosé, in tight shorts that made me resemble a ho.

The barbecue was fabulous! There was so much meat I even had leftovers, which I brought home with me in a doggy bag for Anna. Anna removed her leash and said, "Woof, woof, thank you."

Since after that I was out of doggy bags, I saved some more leftovers in a douchebag and mailed them to Hung and his friends, Hocus/Pocus.

## JUNE 2

*Dear Diary:*

Today is Queens Pride in Jackson Heights! I asked if Anna from Louisiana wanted to join the party I was attending but she said she needed to finish laundry, which meant watching the past ten episodes of *The Biggest Loser*. Anna loves feeling good about herself by watching people fatter than her jiggling on a treadmill. Anna often complains about feeling bloated, but would never work out even if I chained her to an elliptical and put a dildo over her head.

Back to Pride! A former hookup of mine hosts a fabulous yearly brunch in Jackson Heights so I spent the entire day there. I was commando and wore my unusually tight shorts and you could see everything—or so was the hope—and Carlos joined me. Not only did I want to introduce him to my friends, but my ass enjoyed the consensual harassment throughout the day.

Gay men love their parades! For us, parades are like blood for mosquitoes and we can't survive without them. Parades are meaningful, signifying how far we've come. Plus, we wanna show off our shirtless bodies anywhere where it's allowed, so nowhere near Iran.

Drunk, happy, and in love with Carlos, I returned home at close to four in the morning. Summer recharges me like no other season, and every Sunday in June a borough gets a Pride parade—Queens, Brooklyn, Staten Island, the Bronx, and finally Manhattan. Lots to celebrate this month and lots of slutty swimsuits to wear.

Just like I predicted, Anna's whites weren't done but were still soaking in a bucket of bleach, so I added my white shorts into it. They got dirty during the parade because of how dirty I behaved. Like Daddy, like pants!

## JUNE 3

*Dear Diary:*

I'm so hungover because I partied way too much last night. Jackson Heights exploded with gay men and I was having the time of my life. Good luck getting into a bar during Pride. We went to a local bar, Putas, and the line was longer than at a sex shop in Hell's Kitchen when a new flavor of poppers comes out.

Go-go boys in jockstraps danced all night long on top of the bar. Jockstraps are vital to me—during the scorching summer months that's all I wear, and I purchase at least a dozen before each summer season. People often tell me I have a nice, bouncy butt so there's no way I'm hiding my ass in shapeless boxers or baggy pants.

Look, if I wanna see baggy pants I'll just stay an extra hour at work with Hung.

# JUNE 4

*Dear Diary:*

Anna from Louisiana still hasn't paid me the last month's rent and I'm starting to suspect her avoidance of paying and lies are a common theme with her, similar to her stupidity, lack of respect, and her crazy hair everywhere.

Before moving in, Anna swore she'd be cleaning daily as she'd have nothing better to do. The first day she arrived? Anna cleaned one of the stove burners in the kitchen, took a dump, and clogged the toilet. Then, as if nothing happened, she went to her bedroom and closed the door.

That night my plunger sucked like it'd never sucked before.

Anna is so lazy. When she showers she cleans half a boob, and because she refuses to wear deodorant, my apartment gets a certain pungent armpit smell.

I texted that shrew: *"Hi, love bug. The rent for June was due on the first. And you still owe me for May."*

I was in the bathroom when I heard Anna knocking. I washed my hands and came out.

"What's up, Double Ds?"

She said, "I was under the impression that rent is due at the end of the month."

"May ended four days ago. Buy a fucking calendar. The rent is always—always—due on the first. Who was your landlord in the past?"

"My parents."

"So you owe me for May and June. Are you paying cash, through Venmo, with a check, or with poppers?"

Anna fabricated a story that she hadn't been paid from her job yet. Such a liar! Last week at least fifteen packages arrived for her from the internet: five pairs of brown moccasins, three XXXL blouses in polka dot, and a vagina rejuvenator.

I said, "So you don't have the rent money but your Etsy invoice tops the national debt?"

"Those are the essentials."

"What about my essentials, Anna, like Imodium, Diurex, and poppers? What am I supposed to send the landlady?"

Anna shrugged. Later, I stole her vagina rejuvenator and sent that.

## JUNE 5

*Dear Diary:*

I fell asleep on the subway going to work and not one person woke me up. So rude. I used to wake people up often. I would tell them, "Hey, thanks for coming over but it was a hookup and I didn't realize you were sleeping over."

## JUNE 6

*Dear Diary:*

I went to a UPS store to return a package, all along wondering why they call it a UPS "store."

A store is a place where you can purchase some food or a last-minute birthday present. When was the last time you had an emergency and walked to UPS, hoping to buy a gift for your friend's birthday? What will you even say? "Here's some shipping tape, Dakota Johnson. I heard you're into bondage."

Or when was the last time you dropped by UPS to pick up a quick lunch with Titus Burgess? I'm embarrassed by even thinking about what I'd say. "Look, bitch, a UPS store. Their medium-sized boxes are to die for and I lost fifty pounds by juicing them."

The UPS "store" I went to was located on the Upper East Side, extremely small and crowded. Listen, when you're in a tight, crowded space and you see a large package behind the counter, you're not at a store. You're in Jackson Heights at a gay bar.

**JUNE 7**

*Dear Diary:*

Carlos and I have decided to be exclusive! I know it hasn't been a month but we feel ready for a commitment. To celebrate, we had dinner at an Italian restaurant and Carlos ordered himself a pizza with pepperoni, chicken, and sausage.

I like a guy who likes his meat.

I feel like Carlos is the guy for me. Yes, I know I said it every other time, but this one feels different. Carlos *gets* me. And he can get real *deep*, too . . .

. . . feelings-wise.

## JUNE 8

*Dear Diary:*
   Carlos and I went to get some sun at Pier 45.
   Pier 45 is a gay paradise on the west side of Manhattan where gay men and everyone in between come to show off and sunbathe.
   Since I'm insecure about my body, I was wearing a tank top the entire time. I assumed I'd be inspired to work out after seeing all these hunks with golden, leathery, fried-chicken skin. Not at all. The entire time I was just hungry for some fried chicken.

## JUNE 9

*Dear Diary:*
   I'm truly tired of Anna's hair all over the apartment. I'm considering exchanging her for an animal or a piece of furniture. I've never owned anything but a betta fish, so perhaps it's time for something hairier like a cat or dog. At least they don't smell.
   I found a seamstress in Canarsie, Brooklyn, through Craigslist and she said she'd turn all of Anna's hair into a big, fuzzy sweater. When the seamstress sends the sweater back and Anna asks me why it smells, I'll explain, "Because it's made from a skunk."

## JUNE 10

*Dear Diary:*

Went to see movies with my friend Noah. First of all, who the fuck came up with the name Noah? Was his dad going too deep and his mom yelled, "No! Ah!"?

Take the name Oliver, for example—a food connoisseur saw a pâté and shouted, "O! Liver!" and now it's someone's name.

Don't even get me started on Apple and Sunday. Those are not names, those are the reason to call the Child Protective Services. The name Apple is boring, and on Sundays I'm hungover.

I like Gravity as a wacky name, however. I *respect* gravity, because it keeps me grounded.

Anyway, Noah and I saw *Gravity* with Sandra Bullock. Sandra—excuse my French—doesn't do shit! She gets stranded in deep black space and hangs around *thinking* for two hours. What was the budget, two bucks? Where were costumes and props? *Anything?* At the beginning of the movie, I sneaked out and watched porn instead.

Noah was upset that I didn't watch *Gravity* with him, so I said, "Look, I basically watched the movie with you. Sandra was a white woman in deep black space, right? And I watched a white twink gangbanged *deep* by big black men. At least in my movie there were props—pillows, furniture, and dildos!"

## JUNE 11

*Dear Diary:*

My fish Kiki is beyond stupid. When I feed her, she hides in the bush at the bottom of the tank and stays there, lazily waiting until her pellets sink.

Look, I like hiding in the bush like the next gay man, but when Daddy gives you food, you open your mouth and swallow, bitch!


## JUNE 12

*Dear Diary:*

Anna from Louisiana and I were talking about names. She wants to name her daughter Jane.

"Children are bullies!" I told her. "They'll bully the shit out of Jane."

"Why?"

"Because it rhymes with too many words. Jane is vain; Jane likes cocaine; Jane needs Accutane."

"I agree," Anna said. "What would you call yours?"

"First, I must make sure it doesn't rhyme with Taylor, like Gaylord. Syria, Siberia, or Nigeria don't and could all be potential name options."

"But you're Russian," Anna said. "The bullies will say: 'Nigeria has a Russian dad who likes to get dildoes in his butt.'"

I said, "Bullies will be bullies. There's nothing wrong with dildoes up one's butt."

## JUNE 13

*Dear Diary:*

I had a nightmare last night, and I woke up with my heart racing. In the nightmare, Anna from Louisiana paid her rent, and when she used the bathroom she cleaned it instead of clogging it. She brought home three half-used toilet paper rolls from work, which lasted her seven assholes for at least two days. When she made bacon for breakfast she somehow didn't burn it, she stopped complaining about her weight, and used deodorant after a shower.

So. Fucking. Disturbing.

## JUNE 14

*Dear Diary:*

Anna from Louisiana has *finally* paid the last month's rent—six weeks late—with a check.

I said, "Why did it take so long?" and quickly deposited the check with my phone before she spent it all.

She said, "Well, I shopped at a store my bank didn't recognize so they froze my account. So I had to transfer money from one account to another—"

I don't care!!! Just pay me! I felt so impatient I went for a metaphor and politely said, "Listen, bitch. When I take the subway I'm not interested in how it works. I give them business by paying the fare and they make sure it doesn't smell like urine."

## JUNE 15

*Dear Diary:*

Carlos and I went to Brighton Beach to visit my Russian people. Out of respect for my heritage, I come at least twice a year.

The best part about Brighton Beach is the boardwalk, where you can sit at a seedy café, drink beer, and gossip about passers-by in ugly outfits. Russian food tastes fantastic and whatever you order is at your table in two minutes flat. It's quicker than Grindr but for gastronomes.

As for me, those Grindr days are over. It's been a whole month and I don't even remember what Grindr looks like or why people use it. Is Grindr about donuts? Because I recall something about holes being filled.

## JUNE 16

*Dear Diary:*

Holy crap! I just realized Carlos and I have been together a month! We see each other four times a week and talk every hour, so if this isn't love (and lots of anal), I don't know what it is. Plus, we're going to Canada next week for a vacation and I can hardly wait to show him Montreal's bathhouses!

Last year while in Montreal I had sex in a bathhouse, and there's nothing like the irony of getting clean while getting dirty.

## JUNE 17

*Dear Diary:*

I went to the bathroom in the morning...

OMG!

Blood was all over the place! It was all over my pink, fuzzy toilet seat, all over the mirror, and even all over the floor tiles. Red was everywhere you looked! For a second I wondered whether I'd moved to Dallas, Texas or another Republican state.

I asked Anna from Louisiana if Harold Shipman had come over and tried to kill her.

Anna said, "No, I cut myself last night."

"*Cut what?* Your whole arm off?"

"No, just my finger."

"Then why the fuck didn't you clean up?"

"I didn't wanna disturb you by cleaning at two in the morning."

"Disturb me? Anna, I'm on so much Benadryl for my allergies, two elephants—or you—can have sex and I won't wake up."

We had a big, fat (but skinny!) argument and I brought up everything: from her hair everywhere to her clogging up the toilet to her owing me rent.

"Anna, I need the rent money stat. I'm going to Canada with Carlos in a few days, and poutine isn't cheap!"

"I'll have the money on the twenty-second."

"But I'm leaving on the twenty-*first*."

She said, "Yeah, I know."

I'm so furious and hope she burns in hell. Anna is such a baby and never takes any responsibility. If she doesn't clean up her mess or pay her rent, I'm putting her in a huge basket and sending her down the Hudson River. I'm hoping the basket reaches a pair of lovely parents who'll adopt her and, once they realize how horrible she is, kill her.

At least it won't be me!

## JUNE 18

*Dear Diary:*

I receive emails from my plastic surgeon's practice once a week. I'm totally brainwashed by unrealistic expectations of today's culture that promotes youthful appearance above all—and I love it! Fillers and Botox look natural to me, but armpit hair and reusable tampons don't.

The subject line of the email was: *"You can still look good for ten percent off!"*

*Still* look good? I'm only thirty-one . . .

. . . which means the end of the world for a millennial.

Gay men must receive emails from Oprah, plastic surgeons, and personal trainers to remind us that self-improvement is constant work. That's my life and I don't wanna justify it. Yes, I may be ancient and a has-been in the gay world, but I take care of myself by trimming my bush, wearing sunscreen, and eating only when necessary. So what if I get Botox injections once in a while? It doesn't hurt anybody—except my forehead.

By contrast, my straight brother—thirty-three, believes the Earth is flat, eats *every* meal, and thinks sunscreen is for girls—only receives emails from diaper wholesalers and divorce lawyers. *"Divorce cheap and your wife won't even know! Now ten percent off!"*

That's his life, so a nice person shouldn't judge him. But I'm a bitch, so I will!

## JUNE 19

*Dear Diary:*

I'll be brief as I'm packing for Canada. Our flight is tomorrow at eight in the morning, and I must fold five more jockstraps and figure out how to sneak poppers over the border.

## JUNE 20

*Dear Diary:*

The flight to Montreal was a disaster. During the flight—somewhere near Syracuse—the turbulence was so intense the plane started shaking and went up and down as if we were in Disney World on a rollercoaster ride. I thought we were going through Britney Spears' 2007 mental breakdown—up and down, up and down.

But eventually we made it! As did Britney.

Flying makes me hungry so we had lunch right away. I had poutine, which was served on a plate the size of Texas with a massive mountain of french fries drenched in brown gravy and cheese. So. Much. Food. I. May. Never. Eat. Again. Back home we don't call it poutine, we call it Mama June's snack.

Montreal is fabulous so far! During the summer, Saint Catherine Street is closed to traffic in the Gay Village, and they hang these rainbow-colored balls that are suspended above for fifteen blocks. Balls, balls, balls. I haven't seen so many balls since the U.S. Open. You know what else was open all day and balls were involved? Bathhouses.

**JUNE 21**

*Dear Diary:*

Carlos and I went hiking in Mont-Royal. Today is dreadful and cloudy and I was scared we wouldn't take any good pictures. Carlos says in photography lighting is fundamental, but there was no sun for good photos.

I wore a skimpy pair of shorts that hid nothing and made me resemble a rhinoceros in a thong. My butt looked good though: nice and tight and full. I'm sorry, but when you're a medium and you wear an extra small, all the crevices will be filled. That's just good physics.

While climbing the mountain, I was slowly overheating and—proportionally—my penis expanded in my tight shorts (things expand in the heat. Again, just good physics). My crotch looked like I stuffed it with Wentworth Miller.

Look, I just wanted whatever little sun was seeping through to reflect from all of my curves and angles, and photography is all about lighting.

By the time we reached the top, I was sparkling *so* bright, not only did our photos end up terrific—everyone else's too!

## JUNE 22

*Dear Diary:*

Still in Montreal. I would move here in a heartbeat, except everyone speaks French. So rude. When people visit New York I always accommodate them. I've met people from all over the planet and not once have they told me my oral skills are bad.

## JUNE 23

*Dear Diary:*

I love Montreal! Or, rather, I love the currency conversion. We went to a fancy French restaurant for dinner, which would cost an arm and a leg in New York or a fuck-fuck and a suck-suck on Twelfth Avenue at a seedy bar.

You know, expensive restaurants aren't expensive because of better food. They just call themselves French and inflate their prices one hundred percent. I know everything there's to know about inflation—I've blown a hundred balloons in my lifetime, and not only balloons—and prices increase proportionally the closer to a big city you are, even if you order the same thing everywhere. Eventually the food will come back out of you—

straight into the toilet. Was it worth five hundred Canadian dollars? No!

If I eat a slice of pizza in Queens for a dollar, I shit for one day, if I eat a slice of *Italian* pizza in Brooklyn for two dollars, I shit for two days, and if I eat a slice of pizza in Manhattan all of a sudden it's French, costs a hundred dollars, it's no longer called pizza but boeuf bourguignon, and I shit for a week.

## JUNE 24

*Dear Diary:*

Carlos and I rented bikes and schlepped to Parc Jean-Drapeau. I probably misspelled the park's name because French people add extra letters to just about every word. Boeuf bourguignon, anyone?

Everything must be extra for the French—French bread, for example, is called a baguette. *Why?* There are more letters in "baguette" than flour by weight. Do you know what the French call Wonder Bread? They call it "Ew, gross."

The French are real proud and snobby about their bread.

I once slept with a French guy and he was tickled to death when I said, "Oh, baby, your baguette is delicious. Your baguette smells amazing. Your baguette is big and long."

My main breakthrough in Montreal was to learn that I already know how to speak French. I've been saying the word *douche* for years, which is French for "shower." When you see a bottle that says *gel de douche*, that translates to "body wash,"

*Pomme de douche* is a "showerhead," and if you buy a *douchebag*, you bought yourself a "Justin Bieber."

## JUNE 25

*Dear Diary:*

Happy immigration anniversary to me! Exactly twelve years ago I immigrated to the United States and lived in Washington D.C. for a year. I love going down memory lane more than Heather Locklear loves going down on her medication.

In my first year I worked as an Au Pair and it was no fun. I was disappointed when I learned about a crazy guy who was so obsessed with his girlfriend—she was also an Au Pair—that when she was leaving for Brazil he murdered her and the family with whom she lived, all because of love. Nobody ever loved me in such a romantic way. It was always *blah, blah, blah,* hugs, kisses, and presents. Not once has a boyfriend said, "Money or I'll shoot!"

A year later, my wish came true when I lived in East Harlem. It happened in a dark alley and the guy said, "I'm gonna shoot," so I opened my mouth.

## JUNE 26

*Dear Diary:*

OMG! I have some news for you. Guess what Anna from Louisiana had the nerve to do? She moved out while I was on my vacation in Canada (going down on poutine and my boyfriend).

Anna left a note: *"Going to Secaucus to live with my Aunt, Lazy Eye. I will try paying you the money I owe, but there's more chance it'll rain poppers on a Thursday night at seven. Do you know what else you won't be seeing? A skinny face in the mirror after all that poutine, you dumb bitch!"*

What a rude thing to say! I would never bring poutine into this.

I have mixed feelings about this. On the one hand, Anna left and her hair left with her. On the other hand, I had a grilled cheese sandwich and I know that everything will be OK, so long as I continue getting stuffed.


## JUNE 27

*Dear Diary:*

Canadian poutine left me bloated and gassy, so I accidentally farted on the crowded subway coming from work.

I couldn't prevent the gas leak because I was shitting all day and my gas valve was now loose. Someone even notified ConEdison on my behalf. If smoking was allowed, we would have exploded.

Ugh, going back to the routine after a vacation sucks! I haven't had this much sucking since my last threesome.

## JUNE 28

*Dear Diary:*

Today is my palm reader's birthday, and he's a great—though shady and unreliable—gay man. It's either Adam or Josh, I can't remember. But because he's pudgy and weighs close to a hundred and twenty pounds, he *should* have two names.

I purchased him a personal trainer session for seventy bucks at a local gym as a birthday present, but my card was declined so if he still wants to go, he'll have to pay himself. I may be spending too much money on Adam (or is it Josh?), but I love treating my friends well.

I bought him dinner and drinks for his last birthday, but since he was out of town I had the dinner alone. For the birthday before that, I got him a box of chocolates with almonds without realizing he was allergic. So I had to eat the chocolate myself. I'm gaining weight just to please the bastard!

Adam (or Josh) keeps complaining that because he's "gay old," he hasn't had any action in a long time, that he's becoming undesirable, that only bears will have sex with him—blah, blah, blah.

Next year I'm taking him to swim with dolphins, and I'll coach one of the dolphins how to get frisky and prove Adam (or Josh) wrong.

"See?" I'll tell him, "Not just bears, but dolphins will happily have sex with you too. You're getting more deposits in you than my bank account. And when you die and get cremated, I'll spread your ashes the way you spread your butt cheeks: all over town. Happy birthday, tramp!"

## JUNE 29

*Dear Diary:*

Anna from Louisiana just texted me. She says she forgot some food in the pantry and wants me to send it to her.

I rolled my eyes and replied: *"I'll be in Secaucus on Junetember 35, 3069 and drop it off then."*

She replied with a smiling face emoji.

Anna is so fucking rude. Now you want a favor? Who asks for a favor after leaving a person high and dry? High from poppers and dry from the A/C. When I defecate at a gay bar and leave right away, I don't text the owner and say, *"Hey, Mary, call me back when the smell dissipates!"*

## JUNE 30

*Dear Diary:*

Today is World's Pride and everything is inflated: balloons, drink prices, and—unrelatedly—Venezuela's currency.

Carlos and I attended a house party at noon and then went to watch the parade in Manhattan. Gorgeous men and women came from all over the world, which makes sense of the fact that Meat Loaf, Porkchop, and Carrot Top couldn't make it.

The mathematical formula for a Pride Parade is two and a half drag queens, plus three pounds of glitter, times a million abs. The only downside to Pride? There's so much trash afterward, yet nobody notified me the cast of *Jersey Shore* was joining the party.

Speaking of parties; all sorts of sex parties were going on. The most notable one was the Republican Party.

Whoever joined it was fucked.

# JULY

Rehoboth Beach. I forgot to pack my swimming shorts, so I had to buy a pair from a gift shop, and these look huge (and straight) on me!

## JULY 1

*Dear Diary:*

I went to have dinner in Woodside, Queens, with my ex-boyfriend Josh—AKA: Cheater Who Gave Me Gonorrhea. Yeah, we're still friends and I like to get together once in a while to ensure I am continuing to do better than him.

Josh ordered French onion soup and I ordered the soup of the day, which was two dollars cheaper and was also French onion soup.

Our waitress wanted a bigger tip by trying to upsell all sorts of things. "More drinks? Another soup? A pedicure?"

I get it—every business is struggling, so Josh ordered a French pedicure and I ordered the pedicure of the day, which was two dollars cheaper and was also French.

I'm so classy lately.

French.


## JULY 2

*Dear Diary:*

I ordered a bike helmet so Carlos and I can start biking together because I love spending time with him. Quite truly I've never met anyone with whom I feel as comfortable. I love, for example, that in public I can hold his hand (and his dick).

In the past, I tried to impress my then-boyfriends and even hookups: "Look, a whole hand can disappear in my butt!"

I was so needy!

With Carlos I can be myself (but not too much). I haven't shown him what a hellion I can be—*yet!*—but he'll soon fucking see! So far he thinks I'm absolutely normal. It's indeed hard to please, impress, or upstage New Yorkers. You can show up wearing the highest heels and the sluttiest dress, but a gay boy standing next to you will be even higher and sluttier.

## JULY 3

*Dear Diary:*

Carlos invited me to Central Park for, and I quote, "a fun date."

Fun? Where is the fun? I hate Central Park and it's not the park itself that I hate—I hate crowds, and if I wanna see horses, poop, and angry people I'll return to Kazakhstan where my Grandma used to have a homestead.

True story! The homestead was where I spent the majority of my summers growing up. Grandma had a potato field and she made me pick Colorado beetles from the leaves every day. During those hot summers I was on my knees in the potato field every damn day. That's how I learned about the importance of kneepads, which came in handy later in life.

I used to love riding the mare Grandma owned and I learned how to ride it bareback. I would bareback all summer long and once you bareback, you never go back...

Bareback don't crack.

Twenty years flew by and now, at thirty-one, I hate horses and barebacking (it's not barebacking that I hate but the STDs it brings).

So I told Carlos, "Let's avoid Central Park and bike someplace else. And if later we decide to see a horse, we can bike to the East Village and say hello to Sarah Jessica Parker."

## JULY 4

*Dear Diary:*

Today is Independence Day.

Carlos and I are throwing a party at his place on the Upper East Side, and since I'm decorating everything in red, white, and blue, I bought red wine, White Claw, and gave Carlos blue balls by not blowing him.

I was anxious about meeting his friends, but everyone ended up friendly and loved the baby carrots and baba ganoush I'd laid out for them. Nobody had any idea that baby carrots are regular carrots trimmed into smaller pieces.

"Are you sure?" his friend Kandra asked.

I said, "I went to culinary school so I know everything there is to know about carrots and carotene. I also grow eggplants."

"Really?" she asked. "Like on a windowsill?"

"Sometimes on a windowsill or in the kitchen, but mostly in my bedroom with my mouth."

## JULY 5

*Dear Diary:*

I ate so much baba ganoush yesterday that I can't fit into my skinny jeans today. I'm not ready to show up in public looking so bulky so I called out.

Hung picked up the phone. "Hello?"

I said, "Hey, Hung, can you tell our boss I'm not coming in today? I had too much eggplant last night and I'm not feeling well."

"You gays . . ." he said and hung up.

## JULY 6

*Dear Diary:*

Two years ago I took a DNA test to find out about my ancestry and learn what diseases I might develop. I trust a DNA test more than I trust my psychic Mystik (pronounced: mis-TEEK), who told me ten years ago I'd die at twenty-five from syphilis.

For the DNA test, you spit in an empty tube they send you. Since I'm a lady—*naturally*—I didn't have the faintest idea about spitting, so I watched *Titanic* twice just to learn the technique from Jack Dawson. When my test results came back, they said I was one hundred percent Russian and probably uncircumcised. That's not fucking news! Everyone in Astoria knows that!

But today I received another email from them with the subject line: *"Surprise! Horrible news!"*

Listen, if I wanted horrible news, I'd check my savings account.

Like the psychic Mystik, they've predicted my future. They're saying I have a high risk of developing Celiac disease and must lay off gluten, which, they explained, is a protein found in wheat. I guess they failed to predict I went to culinary school and know everything about gluten. Some lazy scientists they are!

Anyhow, avoiding wheat—like pasta, pastries, and bread—is impossible because wheat is in everything on planet Earth. I'm torn between health and my addiction to ramen. Quite frankly I haven't been this torn since I had a traffic cone up my butt.

But I have some good news: there's still some room left on a spaceship that's headed to colonize Mars in 2030, and there's no gluten on the red planet, so I signed up for only a hundred bucks! They gave me no guarantees as they pick at random, but if they pick me I'm gonna miss Carlos.

Do I really have a choice when it comes to my health? I either go to the red planet Mars or go live somewhere else where it's red, like Alabama, Tennessee, or Ed Sheeran's crotch.

## JULY 7

*Dear Diary:*

I didn't feel too well and needed to treat myself with something special—cortisone cream. Humidity is insane in New York City right now and Truth slides up and down my jockstrap as if lubricated. All that rubbing gets my shlong itchy and irritated.

My penis and I have a lot in common (like Daddy, like shlong) and when we're irritated we become bitchy, impatient, and annoying. Truth refused to get up this morning because he was upset that I rubbed him the wrong way yesterday—with my left hand.

Such a drama queen!

**JULY 8**

*Dear Diary:*

I got drunk and started reminiscing about my culinary school days a long, long time ago—2017. My favorite class was learning how to handle fruits and vegetables.

During a jam-making class, my teacher—Creepy Jake—said, "You're doing a really good job with that peach. Did you shave it?"

I said, "Yes, chef. How can you tell?" Could Creepy Jake see through my checkered chef pants?

He said, "I'm from Georgia, so peaches are my specialty. I like to eat peaches raw when they're ripe, shaved, and sweet."

Later that same night a guy from Grindr told me the exact same thing. Sex and cooking have so much in common!

**JULY 9**

*Dear Diary:*

I'm aging at a rapid speed. Next month I'm turning thirty-two and I'll be as ancient as the sun (complete with yellow spots all over the surface) so I'm having an apple martini to keep strong!

Martinis give me courage, Diary. I may be gay and fabulous but I'm also shy. It took me ten years to even try something kinky like having my hands tied up with an iPhone cord. I may be shy and trashy but I'm a multitasker at heart. Just because I'm tied up, it doesn't mean the iPhone can't be charging at the same time.

## JULY 10

*Dear Diary:*

Had dinner with Carlos and my neighbors Jon and Jon. The dinner was at a restaurant in Astoria where Broadway actors come and perform for free. I'm not a Broadway queen like Jon, Jon, and Carlos but I enjoyed the show anyway. I mean, it was a bit *culty*: everyone knew the lyrics to every song, while I knew every menu item and their vodka selection.

Listen, I graduated from culinary school so the actors can sing all they want. All I care about is how to open my own restaurant with an exquisite gay menu that should be excellent, entertaining, and fabulous.

So how can I serve a drag queen?

## JULY 11

*Dear Diary:*

Besides owning a restaurant, I have other business ideas. After watching the documentary *Sour Grapes*, I feel inspired. The documentary was about Rudy Kurniawan who sold ten thousand counterfeit wine bottles, raking in millions of dollars before going to prison. You know why Rudy was incarcerated in the end? Because Rudy didn't share and *I* understand that sharing is caring.

With my plan, everybody benefits: my investors will pool their money together, and with five million dollars in my pocket I'll fly to Hawaii, where I'll happily live for the rest of my life and—in exchange for their investment—send them royalty-free photographs every quarter. At first they'll probably think, "Why do we need more photos of Hawaii?"

To which I'll say, "I hear you, bitches, but the pictures won't be of Hawaii but of my ass."

Now, Diary. How do I write a business plan without using the words "ass" or "bitches"?

## JULY 12

*Dear Diary:*

I'm amazed by how some companies have recently started converting their subscription models from yearly to monthly. My landlady has been doing that for the past thirty years and nobody gives her any credit. No, literally: she only accepts cash.

Some landlords and some utility companies accept credit card payments, charging a two-percent-processing fee, which is so rude.

What if, after paying for your Netflix subscription with a credit card, they called you and said, "By the way, since you didn't pay *cash*, we need to restrict two percent of our content, so you can't watch the finale of *The Vampire Diaries*."

Then your internet provider calls you and says, "That porn clip you're watching? Yeah, bitch, we don't think so. That's our two percent!" and the clip freezes.

And what if you used a credit card at McDonald's? You take a bite from a Big Mac and in the meantime, you notice a ninja's foot flying near your mouth and somehow the foot (he's a ninja, after all) kicks the tomato back to the cook. That's their two-percent-processing fee. Even in an imaginary scenario that seems rude and wrong. You're not getting fast food; you're getting kung fu'd.

## JULY 13

*Dear Diary:*

Note to Self: never—under *any* circumstances—weigh yourself while bloated, gassy, and constipated after having a burger, fries, and two margaritas.

Big mistake.

Big.

Huge.

## JULY 14

*Dear Diary:*

Bastille Day is today, a French holiday, so I'm baffled why we celebrate it here, but, since I'm gay and my French friend Jean-Baptiste-Alphonse invited me to a party, any excuse to celebrate is good enough for me.

I don't need a reason to celebrate; one time I douched and celebrated when Carlos texted me saying: *"I just got off work."*

Bastille Day started when the French stormed the Bastille, and I would too if I were them. If I could fight for something and get a parade out of it, I'm there.

Currently, Bagwis and I are discussing storming into a local coffee shop on Thirty-sixth Street in Astoria. We want pumpkin-spice-latte enemas for anyone, at a fair price, all year long, and we need a parade to support it.

## JULY 15

*Dear Diary:*

I'm tired and hungover after the party last night and work is out of the question. I tried to come up with an excuse and even typed an email to my boss: *"Good morning, Skinny Bitch. I'm unable to work today and it's a funny story—I took my daddy's Viagra instead of my regular vitamin C and poked a hot guy (Steve) in the eye on the subway because my erection lasted for eight hours. I'm taking Steve to the nearest emergency room. Thankfully, he won't be suing me since it turns out I missed his eye and poked him in the butt."*

But who would ever believe I was a top for once?

Then I realized I was off today anyway. Back to sleep!

## JULY 16

*Dear Diary:*

Work was slow today and I was bored. I started googling random things like why Jesus was crucified, how to cure a jock itch, and why a restroom is called a restroom. When was the last time you rested there? For me, it always feels like work because of all the rules: don't flush tampons, don't drop the soap, lift the seat.

You remember when we put Jesus to rest, right? Did we put him into a rest*room*? Was that because he flushed a tampon? I think we would be better humans if we all learned the bathroom etiquette.

P.S. To cure a jock itch: don't scratch, spray the area, and wipe it clean. Basically, care for your shlong similarly to how you care for wood floors.

## JULY 17

*Dear Diary:*

Carlos took me to see another Broadway show called *The Prom*. No, no. *Prom*. Not *Porn*. The show is about a love story of two lesbians. A U-Haul driver sitting next to me said it was a little unbelievable. He's seen it all but he's never seen two lesbians together for one hour and a half without them moving in together. He rated it two stars—one for each nipple.

## JULY 18

*Dear Diary:*

I said, "Alexa, add avocados to my list."

She said, "I've added avocados to your shit list. Why are you mad at them, bitch?"

I said, "I've just learned that avocados are fruit, similar to tomatoes. A *fruit!* Why isn't it sweet then?"

Alexa said, "What else did you learn?"

"That peanuts are not nuts, they're legumes like peas. I also learned Peaches is Beyoncé's nickname when Jay-Z talks nasty to her."

I'm tired of being confused! When my nutritionist—Lindsay Lohan—says to eat less fruit and more vegetables, what am I supposed to do?

Eating healthy is a science!


## JULY 19

*Dear Diary:*

I just finished a documentary about black holes and I'm fascinated. They're massive and they suck everything near them. I texted my neighbor Liam: *"Liam, you won't believe what just happened! I found your twin."*

**JULY 20**

*Dear Diary:*
 It was two hundred degrees today in New York. I got so dehydrated I almost burst into flames when someone was smoking nearby. For lunch, I craved something refreshing to cool off, like a mimosa and a cold salad with grilled peaches.
 I said, "Alexa, add peaches to my list."
 Alexa said, "OK. Added Beyoncé to your playlist."

**JULY 21**

*Dear Diary:*
 "Alexa, what do you call two gay phones having sex?"
 "A homophone."
 That's fucking right! A homophone is a word written or pronounced the same as another but with a different meaning. The word "broke": you broke something *or* you're out of money. Seriously, why do we have homophones? If we're running out of words, make one up!
 *Ghgfyh.*
 Took me one second.
 I detest double meanings because they're confusing. Take the word "asshole," for example. Nobody understands whether to use it to describe an ass, a hole, or my boss. But when you talk astronomy and mention black holes, no questions are asked because you obviously mean Johnny Depp's mouth. (Have you seen his *teeth*? It's like staring at an unplugged TV screen.)
 Don't you hate it when you google the word "turd" and a picture of Kellyanne Conway pops up? Or when I shop for some

roast beef and they just slice me up a pound of Donatella Versace's neck?

We don't need homophones because of people like Donald Trump. He once needed to send a missile to Iraq and asked his advisor, "Where do I send the missile, Kanye? To Kentucky, Kazakhstan, or the Kardashian? They all sound the same to me."

## JULY 22

*Dear Diary:*

The worst homophones are "slot" and "slut." Every time I'm in Atlantic City I feel embarrassed when I tell my friend, "Vladimir, let's play slots," he misunderstands and immediately walks up to the next man he sees and requests money for sex! It's all because of homophones.

Or maybe it's because Vladimir's an escort.

## JULY 23

*Dear Diary:*

I've been thinking all night, wondering why I hate homophones. It's because I like simple things and often reminisce of the '80s when I was born. There was only one flavor of potato chips at a bodega down the street—vodka flavored—and we were grateful.

Now? You name it, it's a flavor: New York Cheddar, Salt & Black Pepper, and even something called Rippled. What kind of a flavor is that? A condom? FYI, salt and black pepper aren't flavors either; they're fucking condiments. The only person who eats Salt & Pepper chips is Mama June because she'll eat anything at a reasonable price. She's economizing to put Honey Boo Boo through Sausage Packing College. I heard this from TMZ, so it must be true.

I wish potato chip companies experimented more. For example, when I visited North Korea and opened a bag of North Korean Barbecue chips, I thought they tasted like communism and unregulated drugs, and when I flew to LA and opened a bag of Anne Hathaway chips, I thought they smelled like bad movies and body odor.

## JULY 24

*Dear Diary:*

I don't understand why doing laundry is more expensive than buying groceries. If you drop off your laundry at my local Laundromat it costs ninety-nine cents per pound, and cum-stained sheets weigh a ton, so now I just swallow to prevent overspending.

The government subsidizes meat, right? Since I'm in a relationship I get my meat for free. But I don't have a laundry machine in my apartment so I need my *laundry* subsidized. At ninety-nine cents per pound, each load costs twenty bucks. If I wanna pay twenty bucks for a load, I'll hire an escort from Grindr.

At my next meet-and-great with the governor, I wanna bring up real issues like laundry, or why Renée Zellweger's face looks tighter than my ass before my first round of poppers.

## JULY 25

*Dear Diary:*

Carlos came over and we watched *Street Food* on Netflix about Ho Chi Minh City.

I hate it when cities and bridges change their names. Triboro Bridge in New York became RFK Bridge, Saigon became Ho Chi Minh City, and Johnny Depp became a pirate. So when they say "Miss Saigon" they mean it literally. They fucking miss it.

I remember when Constantinople became Istanbul, and it made sense because there were fewer letters to write, which saved space in their local newspaper. I would've shortened it to Dump to be honest. Mumbai used to be Bombay, and Guangzhou used to be Canton. Shouldn't we be consistent and change other names too? Los Angeles to Peligro de Incendio (Fire Hazard), New York to New Jerusalem, and we don't rename Anchorage, Alaska, but sell it back to the Russians.

## JULY 26

*Dear Diary:*

I was researching town names. Some states deliberately came up with the most boring names to upstage other states and make some lists, like:

The most boring city: Freeport City, Kansas.

The least populated city: Freeport City, Kansas (five people).

The city with the most incest: Freeport City, Kansas.

After all, there's no such thing as bad publicity, right? Try to google Climax, Georgia; No Name, Colorado; and Boring, Maryland. I'm asleep! Whoever came up with these boring, unoriginal names have no imagination.

Visit gay-sounding towns like Intercourse, Pennsylvania; Rough and Ready, California; and Mud Butte, South Dakota. I'm not proud of the last one because it started with a messy bottom—his butt was muddy—then when the French took over South Dakota, they added the letter E at the end because they're classy and French, but Butte is not pronounced "butt"; the French say "Booty" instead.

There are also lesbian towns in the United States: Bumpass, Virginia (a spin-off from Bum*puss*, West Virginia). Also lesbian: Bee Lick, Kentucky; and Lick Fork, Virginia.

Don't worry. Even bisexuals are on the map: Needmore, Texas; Peculiar, Missouri; and Truth Or Consequences, New Mexico.

Straight people have everything else: Normal, Illinois; Plain City, Utah; and Why, Arizona.

## JULY 27

*Dear Diary:*

Carlos and I said those long-awaited three words to each other. No, not "fuck me harder" but "I love you." It felt as natural as a ring from Tiffany's on my finger.

I know I love him. I look at him the way I look at sugar-free cookies—with lots of trust and passion. Listen, sugar is bad for you because it goes straight to your ass and face, and if I want it in my ass and face I don't need cookies, I have Carlos.

## JULY 28

*Dear Diary:*

Do you know how I know I'm in love? Today, after smoking some Gorilla Glue #4, I saw a mouse in the kitchen. I asked the mouse to hang out with me instead of throwing a dildo at it like I've done in the past. Pigeons joined us as well, like in *Cinderella*, and we watched *Pretty Woman* and sniffed poppers.

Everything feels amazing! I feel high, not only because I'm high, but because I'm in love. When I went out for some barf bags, the bounce in my step sent out such intense seismic activity that the subway was suddenly on time. Even Hurricane Moon Unit and Hurricane Diva Muffin changed their course and went back to South America.

We're so cute together, Carlos and I, all lovey-dovey. I can't wait until we start fighting though, because I wanna show Carlos some of my moves!

## JULY 29

*Dear Diary:*

Love is blinding and I forgot about the entire world, including the bag of hairiness named Anna from Louisiana, my previous roommate. So when I thought of her I texted her to see how she was doing. I politely asked: *"Where's my money, you dirty whore?"*

She sent me a long text saying she doesn't have it (and it's not *it*. It's plural, bitch! Five hundred dollars' worth of plural).

Anna said, *"I'm working on it day and night."*

I said, *"Where? At Whores R Us?"*

I can smell her lies just I could smell her ripe armpits. Catching a liar is easier than catching syphilis and since I'm a gay man I know what I'm talking about, trust me.

So I must say goodbye to my money forever. Just like investing in Kodak I'd made a bad judgment investing in Anna, a total loss and waste of my time. I should've seen Anna was a psycho after finishing the first season of *You*. Anna had no social media, friends, or a real job as a panty designer. She lied about everything!

At least I can deduct her from my taxes next year and write her off as a loss of rental income. From now on, if you wanna live with me, either have an excellent credit score or a huge dick, whichever is bigger.

## JULY 30

*Dear Diary:*

I'm ready to forgive Anna, and by "forgive" I of course mean "block her number" and her mom's number too (who, by the way, texted me the other day as if we're friends).

Listen, Mama of Anna from Louisiana, my friendship with your daughter is over. I hate to sound bitter but I don't like losing money, especially when I'm seventy thousand dollars in debt, so if you text me I better hear: *"By the way, Anna just had a botched surgery and looks like Jocelyn Wildenstein."* Or *"Anna has three STDs and a smelly vagina."* Or *"What's your address again? We're sending you a check for two thousand dollars, plus a gift card to Olive Garden, and a bottle of rosé."*

## JULY 31

*Dear Diary:*

The last day of July got me horny. Can you even blame me, Diary? Hot guys in tank tops walk everywhere and by "everywhere" I of course mean "gay bars." The countdown to my birthday begins tomorrow and every day will be a reminder that I'm an old crone.

I said, "Alexa, how much is a new hip?"

Alexa said, "New, thirty thousand. Used, fifteen thousand. At the cemetery, free—but you have to dig. Should I order a shovel?"

"Yes, but order it from Delaware. There's no sales tax."

Look, even dogs know: once they turn ten the jig is up. They stop playing fetch because there's nothing fetch about being ten. Once I turn thirty-two (or a hundred in gay years), I know one thing will be true: I'll need a sitter who can change my diapers and who can feed me from a spoon. But where will I find the money for the sitter? Should I just take out another loan? The end is near anyhow so why not live life to the fullest?

I said, "Alexa, since I'm dying soon, order me everything from my list."

Alexa said, "OK, bitch. I'm ordering five cheesecakes, a used hip from Delaware, and a traffic cone from Discreet Adult Toys R Us. Also, have a good day!

# AUGUST

#TBH. Are those shorts or a skirt??? SMH.

**AUGUST 1**

*Dear Diary:*

Carlos gave me the keys to his apartment!!! Do you know how happy I am right now??? On a scale of New York neighborhoods from Tuckahoe, Bronx to the Upper East Side, I'm somewhere in between on Randall's Island, and I'm happy not only because Carlos trusts me but because I can come over while he's at work and steal his toilet paper.

I'll start sending packages to his place because my building is not as secure. The last time when I ordered something from the internet, some cunt stole my package and three dildos that were inside. I guess what a pussy really needs is just a dildo.

Lastly, I just love taking dumps at Carlos's bathroom because his plumbing is top-notch. After living with Anna from Louisiana, my toilet is no longer the same. She flushed her tampons and who knows what else inside the toilet bowl, making my plunger work harder than my douche.

So, yes, long story short, I'm super excited about his keys!

**AUGUST 2**

*Dear Diary:*

I've been constipated since Sunday and today got high on laxatives alone. I take so much Imodium to treat diarrhea and laxatives to treat constipation that my body is confused about what it's supposed to do.

To shit or not to shit? That is the question.

So this week my colon had finally had enough and was like, "Nuh-uh, Sweet Cheeks, I'm so tired of this. No more shit with me!"

I decided to give my body a rest and go the natural route, so I tuned in to FOX News—they always give me the shits.

## AUGUST 3

*Dear Diary:*

This morning Carlos told me I snore like an excavator and, of course, I took it very personally.

Excavators don't snore. If you're trying to insinuate I grunted in my sleep, it's because I had a dream about lifting weights. If you mean I sounded as if I was snorting like a pig, well pardon me for having a little imagination and having fun. It's eight hours of lying in one spot and I get easily bored or eight hours of sitting in one spot if you're on a plane. (My friend Paula Deen said Rosa Parks wasn't an activist either. She was just exhausted and fell asleep on that bus and *also* snored.)

While we were having this conversation, Carlos also said that I toss and turn so much I should rename myself to Tina Toss'n'Turner and go rolling down the river.

I wish Carlos heard himself in his sleep. He's so quiet and motionless that half the time I wake up with a heart attack, afraid he's dead. There's no twisting, no turning, no action whatsoever. If I wanted no action, I'd sleep with an old Republican.

There are some things you don't say and some things you don't do. I don't wear my bad clothes on Good Friday, I don't wear white after Labor Day, and I certainly don't wear deodorant while in Brooklyn.

**AUGUST 4**

*Dear Diary:*

Tried to educate myself and went to the MET with my *"beast"* friend, Steve (yes: *beast!* If you'd seen his pubes you'd understand).

I'm obsessed with Egypt and its history, which means I watched one documentary and now an expert on pyramids and the Nike. Sorry, I meant the *Nile*. So easy to confuse the two.

Did you know you can get lost in the MET? Somehow I took a wrong turn and ended up in a gay bar. What can I say? I'm a gay man and take my social activities seriously.

The MET is basically an IKEA but with one exception: at the MET, when you have lunch, you don't have a cartful of unassembled furniture and there's no Swedish frozen yogurt running down your face.

Unless you hooked up with a Swede on the third floor near the European wing, then yes, you have something white running down your cheek.

**AUGUST 5**

*Dear Diary:*

Instead of grocery shopping I went sex-toy shopping. Since I'm on a strict diet of sucking Carlos, I don't eat anything else. My birthday is coming up in sixteen days and I wanna look tan, toned, and skinny.

At the sex-toy store I purchased a whip and when I got home I whipped some sense into my internet router. The router has been so naughty lately and the internet constantly goes in and out. When you encounter so many ins and outs, it's no longer the internet but inter*course*.

**AUGUST 6**

*Dear Diary:*

Looked up different internet providers in my area and there are none—zero—zilch—zippo. What is *happening* in Astoria? First, there are no tops anywhere on Grindr for a hookup, and now no internet providers for some healthy competition. What's next? No dark rooms at seedy bars? I'm not OK with that life!

FYI, there's one top left and I snagged him, hoes!

**AUGUST 7**

*Dear Diary:*

I'm still on my pre-birthday diet, so for breakfast I scrambled some cotton balls and dusted them with a sugar-free substitute.

They tasted like macaroons and were light and airy. Tomorrow I'm making cotton-round pancakes.

To be thorough, I went through the fridge and tossed anything with more than seven calories. It means I finally threw out my ex who's been in the freezer since 2018. I left him there because I couldn't finish him in one sitting. He was Finnish and I couldn't finish. So much irony, I can't even.

## AUGUST 8

*Dear Diary:*

That was a joke yesterday about my Finnish ex-boyfriend. What I had in my freezer were some fatty pork ribs which reminded me of him.

The cotton-round pancakes were magnificent! A little dry on the inside but at least I'm detoxing my system. With so much cotton in my body it feels like Rumba is cleaning my intestines.

My next mission is to eliminate coffee from my diet so no more coffee-douching. Coffee has five calories which is too many already, but my morning cold brew comes with milk—another fifty calories wasted. If regular milk is unavailable, I milk Carlos.

I don't have an eating disorder. By losing weight I'm also saving homeless children, endangered animals, and the Amazon rainforest. I'm not sure how yet, but if Mother Teresa starved to help the world, then so will I.

## AUGUST 9

*Dear Diary:*

Carlos rented a car and we went to Rehoboth Beach for the weekend. Since the drive was four hours, Carlos was teaching me basic Spanish.

*"Chúpame"* means "hello."

*"Pasivo"* means "good morning."

*"Activo"* means "good evening."

Carlos is delightful. He wants me to know what to say in case I quit my stupid job and start working at a restaurant. Carlos knows the kitchen in New York can be very Hispanic. I can't wait for my first day. I'll tell everyone, *"Chúpame,* whores! Let's cook up a storm!"

## AUGUST 10

*Dear Diary:*

The beach was fabulous. I'm not thrilled about the sand—it gets fucking everywhere—but we took drinks with us so I stopped complaining. What can I say? I'm gay and need my mouth occupied at all times.

At the beach, I tried burying myself in the sand. I'm old and need to research how it feels to live in a grave for the rest of eternity. Not too bad. As long as I can take a drink with me to the other side I'm sure the afterlife will be great.

## AUGUST 11

*Dear Diary:*

We're on the way back from Rehoboth Beach and there's heavy traffic. For lunch, I made the mistake of ordering french fries and a baked tilapia at a diner—at a *diner*—what was I thinking?

The good news is I'm alive. Right after eating, the tilapia swam through my colon toward my anus in one piece and exited back into the wild.

Then we left for New York.

The bad news is the french fries are about to shoot out of me too, and we're on New Jersey Turnpike without a single rest stop in sight. What is more appropriate after four months of dating? To shit one's pants or stick one's butt out of the car's window?

I went for the number two.

(See what I did there?)

## AUGUST 12

*Dear Diary:*

My female neighbor from upstairs was so loud moving furniture that I couldn't concentrate on having sex with Carlos. Who moves furniture at one in the morning? Yes, I know, I once did it at three. But it wasn't *one!* Trust me, two hours make a significant difference when it comes to many things, especially if you're two hours late for work. Is my neighbor from Colorado and forgot to change her clock from Central Time?

I need revenge!

**AUGUST 13**

*Dear Diary:*

What kind of revenge can I take on the loud hussy upstairs? It's not like I can turn on the water and flood her fucking apartment. We've never met, so I imagine her as ugly and stupid like Anna from Louisiana. My imagination gives me comfort because when you imagine what someone looks like, *you're* in control.

For instance, I've never met my next-door neighbor either, but I know she's vanilla because she's *incredibly* loud in bed (which means nobody gagged her mouth the way I like mine gagged).

I've also never met the guy from across the airshaft because he keeps his shades half-closed. I can only see his muscular legs and the guys who are on their knees.

**AUGUST 14**

*Dear Diary:*

Finally took my revenge on the upstairs neighbor who moves her fucking furniture at three in the morning.

I didn't come home tonight, you dumb bitch! Suck on that!

## AUGUST 15

*Dear Diary:*

Last night's revenge was not nearly enough.

Some asshole guru said, "Kill them with kindness," but I'm Russian, and if I send her kindness—or what I call the counterfeit vodka I purchase from my dealer Vladimir—she'll die. She's all moved in anyhow and stopped shifting her furniture around. If she dies a new person will have to move in and the whole process will start all over. Sometimes you must accept your losses, and if you think your neighbor is too loud you're not a real New Yorker.

I don't wanna act like a high school bitch, making her life miserable. After I purchased some earplugs everything is OK, and if her apartment burns down while she's at work . . .

You can't always blame it on me, right?


## AUGUST 16

*Dear Diary:*

Carlos and I went to Beacon, New York, for some hiking. Don't mix Beacon, New York, with Bacon, New York, where you can only hike to a local deli for a BLT.

Beacon is cute, small, and easy to navigate—basically a replica of me. Of course, hiking up a mountain in six-hundred-degree weather wasn't easy and we drank so much water my sodium and potassium levels are out of whack. We finished the day with class by having tapas at a charming café on Main Street, where I had guacamole and sore feet.

My smartwatch marked twenty-four thousand steps, which is hard to check for accuracy. Do you actually believe a dwarf is sitting inside my watch with a pedometer, counting my steps? If he does then he's a loser. If you need a job that badly, suck someone off in an alley behind my apartment building, and don't forget to text me so I can have a glass of wine and watch from my window.

## AUGUST 17

*Dear Diary:*

After hiking yesterday, I'm more exhausted than I was back in 2014 after a *churrascaria* (the word for a Brazilian barbecue).

*Churrascaria* is when waiters walk around with skewers of various meats and dump the meat straight on your plate. There's more dumping at *churrascaria* than at Octomom's house after some spicy Mexican.

Here's how it works: you pay a fixed price—like a hundred bucks—and eat as much meat as you want. My friend Nikita and I tried to get our money's worth and spent five hours there. Sometime during hour two I trained our waiter Pedro to cut the meat from the skewer and toss it straight in my mouth as if I were a seal. In the end he gave us five dollars off because we didn't dirty up any plates.

My point is, after all that walking in Beacon I lost the required weight for my birthday!

## AUGUST 18

*Dear Diary:*

I got a pimple today, five days before my birthday. It's my karma for thinking of taking revenge on my upstairs neighbor by sending her a letter with magazine cutouts that says: "I KNOW WHAT FURNITURE YOU MOVED LAST SUMMER, YOU LOUD FLOOZY!"

Look, I'm trying to keep it friendly in the building by sending threats to everyone, but clearly touching a magazine I stole from another neighbor didn't benefit me at all. Fine, assholes, I will sleep on the Upper East Side with my boyfriend again.

I'm also constipated after eating too many cotton balls the past week. I have more cotton inside of me than a Macy's.


## AUGUST 19

*Dear Diary:*

I binged on the entire season of *Big Ang*, and I'm obsessed because she reminds me of my mother who lives in Russia. I'm always drawn to mother figures like Big Ang, Mother Theresa, or Mama June. Not that I think Mama June is a great mother. I just, in general, love people who are more fucked up than I am.

Big Ang is different, though. She loves drinking, plastic surgery, and big boobs. I wish my mother was similar and cared for topics that are dear to me.

But that's the ugly truth: we want what we don't have. It's a double-edged sword, really, because my mom wishes her gay son was straight and married with kids like my brother, but she also wishes her straight son was prettier and smarter like me.

## AUGUST 20

*Dear Diary:*

In Russia it's my birthday, because they're thirteen hours ahead. Plus, I like to celebrate twice and love everything in pairs regarding birthdays, presents, or martinis.

Double is back in fashion! For example: if you're a couple you save money on rent and groceries, but also on condoms because you use none. Married couples also save on taxes. If you're a gay couple (like Carlos and me), you wear each other's clothes, saving millions on your wardrobe. Besides, after the initial investment—expensive dates, slutty underwear, and trips to Canada's bathhouses—dating eventually stops and hibernation (and savings) begin.

Compare it to being single: you pay for Netflix, dildoes, and an apartment all on your own—at least that's how it was for me.

Do you know what else I like double? No, not double penetration—that's *old* news—I'm talking about double birthday celebrations. Goldilocks was the perfect example: celebrating for a month is too much, once is too little, and twice is just right.

To make sure I weigh even less for tomorrow, I douched once more and my scale was at a hundred and forty-nine pounds! Not too much. Not too little. Just right.

## AUGUST 21

*Dear Diary:*

Today is my birthday! Under normal circumstances I'm thirty-two and skinny, but under gay circumstances I'm the sperm whale—big, ancient, and full of sperm.

While my straight friends say how young I look, my snarky gay friends ask me whether my walker's size is small, medium, or large. Right, like I'd wear a *large*. The brazen ones even ask for homework tips. "Hey, I'm doing a history assignment. How was Lincoln in real life?"

Can you imagine? FYI, Lincoln was fine but I hated his cologne. Actually, I just hated how slow he was. It took the bitch four months to get to Delaware and three weeks to get to his own funeral. Was he taking the Z Train from Brooklyn?

To celebrate my thirty-second, my friends took me to a German pub where we stuffed ourselves with schnitzel and sausage.

Question: how many gay men does it take to eat a sausage? Well, let me put it this way. There were seven of us, but only one swallowed.

**AUGUST 22**

*Dear Diary:*

I'm upset! I just learned that Big Ang died four years ago at only fifty-five from throat cancer. Ugh, everyone's dying on me, which is unfair. The only mother I have left in the United States is Mama June, and calling her a mother is a stretch, just like her cellulite.

## AUGUST 23

*Dear Diary:*

My neighbors—Jon and Jon—invited me over for a movie and dinner, which meant I was invited for five bottles of red wine and some kiki. I haven't seen them all summer because I've been mostly on the Upper East Side with Carlos, and it was nice "catching up"—slang for drinking and bitching.

I told them all about Anna from Louisiana and how I'm still finding her hair on the kitchen rug two months later. Her hair is everywhere, like the news about the Kardashians—you simply can't escape.

Jon and Jon bitched about their problems: their seventeen-thousand-dollar dresser (eye roll) from Williams-Sonoma was delayed for five weeks.

"Seventeen thousand?" I asked, flabbergasted.

"Well, almost eighteen," Jon said.

I asked, "Delayed because of what? Is there a shortage of fine trees on Venus I didn't know about? Did you ask Elon Musk if he could personally deliver your dresser on a flying Tesla?"

Jon said, "Yeah, he's busy."

But that's the whole point: Jon and Jon don't understand my problems, and I don't understand . . . *my* problems either.

## AUGUST 24

*Dear Diary:*

To further educate myself, I watched a documentary about interracial relationships today. Only they didn't call it a documentary, they called it porn. Listen, it's not about what you call it but about how much you learn from it, and today I learned that "interracial" means "hot and big," so if anyone asks, I watched a documentary about the sun.

## AUGUST 25

*Dear Diary:*

I did "Landry" today, which is my slang for doing "laundry." It started when my coworker Hung invited me for drinks and I texted back, saying I was doing laundry.

Hung retorted with: *"You? Laundry? Ha! You mean, Landry?"* followed by a winking emoji.

Please, under *no* circumstances send a winking emoji, you Republican freak in khaki pants!

For whatever reason, Hung thinks my life is so fabulous that my clothes either clean themselves like a cat or that I'm so rich that I have a housekeeper, Rosario, who does my laundry for me. Hung thinks all I do as a gay man is have sex in seedy bars and that's not *all* I do.

Sometimes I have sex in nice bars too.

I'm not sure how to relay to Hung that I still have chores as a human, a Democrat, and a boyfriend. Dishes must be washed, boyfriends sucked off, and President Trump impeached.

I'm fucking busy!

## AUGUST 26

*Dear Diary:*

For our three-month anniversary, Carlos and I confabulated for hours about us. Things are getting serious so we talked about living together. I already spend four nights at his place and he spends three at mine. We're so inseparable that he's Tiffany to my Co.

I haven't lived with a boyfriend since I was twenty-two, quite literally ten years ago. How does it even work? Do we live in my two-bedroom in Astoria and pay less, or do we stay in his studio on the Upper East Side and pay twice as much?

We realized it would be foolish to decide now, as it may be a year or more before we commit, but if we move in together I'll ask Carlos to flip for it—heads: my place, tails: his—only we'll do it on the trick coin with no tails that I purchased in Vegas, so he's stuck in Astoria. A winking emoji is appropriate here, by the way.

## AUGUST 27

*Dear Diary:*

Six days later and I finally finished the present Carlos got me for my birthday, a book by Brené Brown. I'm such a slow reader. I'm the opposite of a bookworm because I love rereading the same book dozens of times until pages are worn and (only sometimes) stained with drool or cum. I mostly read on my Kindle, so if it's drool or cum, it's someone else's from the subway.

Brené's book was about being courageous and vulnerable at work, and I realized why I'm so miserable there—because I'm neither.

With some rare exceptions, people are easily replaceable. If you're an employee you're supposed to express happiness, and if you complain you appear small, stupid, and vulnerable. Anything you say to the sir sounds like bullshit. You're late because of traffic? The boss doesn't care you live two hours away—just be on time.

So where does that leave me, Diary, with the job that I hate?

## AUGUST 28

*Dear Diary:*

I've been thinking more about Brené's book.

Ten years ago I made twelve bucks an hour. After three years at the job, I asked my boss for a one-dollar-an-hour raise. You know what his response was? He said, "I think you're making enough. How do you think people on minimum wage live?"

Are you seriously asking me how they *live*? They live with their parents or with thirty roommates. They eat ramen because they can't afford real food and they get wasted because they hate their lives.

The minimum wage was seven twenty-five at the time,[1] so I left that job the very next day because life is short.

My patience is precisely like my asshole: there's only so much it can take.

[1] See? I told you I was old. Only I don't think of myself as old. I use adjectives like cool, antique, or refurbished. Oh, who the fuck am I kidding? I'm basically a dinosaur.

## AUGUST 29

*Dear Diary:*

Three days later and I'm still on this whole boss-employee issue. After I quit that job, I went to work at a furniture store in Colorado. I'll try to be discreet like straight guys on the DL because I don't want people to stalk my past, so I'll rename the store: UKEA, a Scandinavian store where they serve Yiddish meat squares.

I remember how much fun it was working there. My manager would start the day by saying, "Hey, good job yesterday, skinny ho!"

The only time anyone else offered me that sentence was a Grindr hookup.

I was thriving and blossoming at that job because I knew my responsibilities, just like I knew my responsibilities with the hookup.

Today, though, I'm entirely lost where my life is taking me. When I was offered lots of money by my previous employer, I quit UKEA and moved back to New York, and I've been at my job ever since, mostly stagnating.

But my boss is feeling stingy again after I asked for a small raise. I'm not buying a condo! All I want is a new dildo, which is in my Amazon cart.

What is it about my boss that makes him appreciate me more only after I quit?

## AUGUST 30

*Dear Diary:*

I'm on my third martini because I'm still upset about my job. The thing is, if I quit I won't qualify for unemployment insurance and won't be able to pay four thousand dollars a month in bills, but if I stay I'll lose my mind.

So what should I do? Drink, obviously.

I'm drunk! You know who we don't celebrate enough? Ruth Bader Ginsburg! During her entire career she's worked for eliminating gender-based stereotyping in legislation, and what have I accomplished? Nothing!

I'm gonna learn more about her but first, one more martini.

Hold on, I'm googling Ruth Bader Gettysburg.

Wait, my bad. Gettysburg is the town in Pennsylvania where Lincoln delivered his address, ginseng is an aphrodisiac and helps with erectile disjunction, and Ginsburg is the Supreme Court justice. I love her already! You can trust *anyone* whose name starts with "gin."

Now compare that to Republican names: Kellyanne CONway, DICK Cheney, and Jeff FLAKE.


## AUGUST 31

*Dear Diary:*

I can't believe August has slipped away, but I do notice a change within me. After Carlos entered me and my life, I no longer hate people because I no longer hate myself. Carlos showed me how valuable I am. Why couldn't I see it in myself before him?

Since 2019 started, I've lost weight, I eat better, and all I need right now is to have enough courage to quit my job. Brené Brown, please help me be courageous, but if I quit, *somebody* has to pay for poppers, and Carlos is too young to be my sugar daddy—at least, that's what he told me after I asked.

# SEPTEMBER

It was fucking freezing today at seven a.m., so I'm wearing a jacket and a hoodie. But I wanted to show off my legs in my whore-shorts somehow.

## SEPTEMBER 1

*Dear Diary:*

Carlos and I went upstate New York for a couple of days to visit his friend Allison. Shouldn't she technically be Allidaughter?

Anyhow, Labor Day weekend is upon us so I'm saying goodbye to my white pants in which I look like a total whore. Until next season, you tight slut!

I helped Allison set up and organize the party and I realized I'm good at event planning. I host fabulous parties like the Fourth of July, birthdays, and threesomes (before my exclusive relationship with Carlos). Maybe one of these days, I'll work as an event planner. I'll even have an ad on TV: "Disappointed in your last party? I bet you didn't have a drag queen or a glory hole at your event."

Did you know that in the good old days, Labor Day was spelled "Labour" Day with the letter U? That's why all other holidays are now U-less—Presidents' Day, Thanksgiving, and even Christmas—we don't have time for extra letters. We're not French.

## SEPTEMBER 2

*Dear Diary:*

I've been so tough on the French lately, and since I hate sounding bitter I wanna clear the air. It's nothing personal. I also hate the Russians, Volkswagen vans, and El Paso, Texas. When you hate yourself, you hate everyone else in your vicinity, and I hate my pathetic existence because of my job and I'm taking the accumulated anger out on just about anyone. Mama June would know.

My French friend Jean-Baptiste-Alphonse doesn't make it any easier to like him. What's up with smoking nonstop, cigarette after cigarette, further trashing the planet and killing the turtles. Or was it children? Some kind of animal . . . Anyhow, smoking is not nice. Plus, he bakes his own baguettes and can't stop talking about them. Enough already, we get it! You like baguettes. Can we talk about *me* for a second? I'm trying to impact the world by not using condoms with Carlos to eliminate plastic and save the fucking turtles. Your baguettes are the last thing on my mind.

When greeting you, Jean-Baptiste-Alphonse blows air kisses, spreading his germs all over the fucking place! In my book, blowing air and spreading germs are the worst! Blow dick and spread your ass cheeks—*that's* nice.

## SEPTEMBER 3

*Dear Diary:*

I found more hair that belongs to Anna from Louisiana, the bitch who used to live with me three months ago. How is her hair still here?

All day today I cleaned and my vacuum sucked, and then we switched. Will burning sage help rid of her stupid spirit?

I burned some sage (literally burned it while making sage chicken) so Anna's spirit should have left the apartment and returned to Secaucus. Lesson learned: never bring a girl, a wool scarf, or anything that sheds into my apartment. Only guests with trimmed bushes are welcome from now on.

## SEPTEMBER 4

*Dear Diary:*

I get Britney now. When she was my age she was not a girl, not yet a woman, and it bothered her. I've just realized I'm at such a stage in my life that I'm not a twink, not yet a bear.

Is there a category I could potentially fit in, like a twink-bear hybrid? A twear? As you can tell, I'm obsessed with multitasking and love merging and abbreviating words to save time. When gay men are cruising on Grindr there's no time for five words, "What are you into sexually?" Instead, you say, "Into?" and send them your address.

I barely have time for douching, let alone typing "double penetration and traffic cones" into the search field on porn sites.

But to be clear, I hate the word "POTUS," but only because it rhymes with "lotus," and that's my least favorite position during yoga or sex—tricky as hell.

## SEPTEMBER 5

*Dear Diary:*

Tennessee Ernie texted me today out of the blue: *"Hey, I need your hole."*

I replied: *"My hole is taken!"*

*"Take the traffic cone out and give me a blow job."*

*"All my holes are closed, Ernie—the jig is up."*

*"My name's Justin. Gimme a hand job at least?"*

*"No, I'm in a relationship now."*

*"Cool, bro. Text me when your hole is back in business."*

Did I ever tell you that Tennessee Ernie was bisexual? His reply to anything used to be, "Cool, bro." He's always cool, thanks to the Gorilla Glue #4 strain of weed.

Regardless, I was happy to learn I'd made such an impact on someone's life. He'd saved my phone number and thought of me when he felt lonely, and here I thought I couldn't impact anyone!

Next, let's save those whales or turtles or whatever the fuck we are saving!

## SEPTEMBER 6

*Dear Diary:*

I was so humbled yesterday by Tennessee Ernie's lovely text. Turns out, when I'm not bitter I love everyone, and today I love bisexuals. They have so much choice, and sex for them must be like a menu at a diner. You can order just about anything. Anything goes. Vagina? Sure, coming right up. Ass? You want it well, medium, or raw? What about some sausage? We have Russian, Polish, and uncircumcised.

Today I don't even mind my French friend Jean-Baptiste-Alphonse. When he texted me: *"Come over at six for baguettes, liver pâté, and fancy French wine,"* instead of saying my routine, *"Fuck you, bitch,"* I said, *"Sure!"*

I learned on Twitter today that loving yourself is step one to getting what you want. My self-esteem is through the roof! I've lost weight, I have a boyfriend, and the French no longer bug me. What is going on? Am I becoming . . . nice?


## SEPTEMBER 7

*Dear Diary:*

I was typing "Kardashians" and realized there's no dash on the keyboard. Why the fuck is that? I had to write Kar--ians with two hyphens instead.

Hold on, googling . . . How do you say it? Is it "hyphen" or "hymen"?

Just learned the difference, and two hymens don't create a dash, FYI. They make two virgins.

Was there no space left on the keyboard to add one dash? We have useless punctuation, letters, and numbers on the keyboard: the colon, the number five, and the letter Z.

The colon is homophonous with intestines—the colon—and you know how much I hate homophones. I also despise the number five. You can't divide five by two to an even number, and odd numbers scare me—trust me, threesomes can be tough to handle. And the letter Z is simply dull! When was the last time when someone was sleeping you didn't see some ZZZs? Boringgggg (with five Gs).

Hmm, maybe the number five isn't that bad, after all.

## SEPTEMBER 8

*Dear Diary:*

TMZ reported this morning that in one year Mama June spends two of my salaries on drugs. TMZ didn't disclose which drugs, but if Mama June is anything like me, I assume Imodium, Gas-X, and poppers.

## SEPTEMBER 9

*Dear Diary:*

After another unsuccessful conversation with my boss about a raise, I had to get a different kind of raise—high.

Right now all I want is to resemble the universe: I wanna *matter*. Did you see what I did there? The universe consists of matt—never mind.

I wanna have a massive black hole in the center, and I want planets to spin around me like lazy Susans, except not lazy.

In my universe, I wanna have the following planets: Uranus and Myanus; Neptunes and iTunes; and Venus and Penus. Six is enough. I'm not the solar system (or my boss), so I'm not greedy.

Before I went to sleep, I took a Benadryl and called out via text: *"Not feeling well. My stomach is in knots."*

My boss replied, *"Lay off Brussel sprouts for a while. You were real gassy today and a client complained."*

## SEPTEMBER 10

*Dear Diary:*

President Donald Duck, I mean Trump, has made over fifteen thousand false claims since taking office in 2016. How is that even possible? He's been in the White House for one thousand days, so that's like what? OMG. Fifteen. False. Claims. A day!

Even I—a great liar—can't come up with so much bullshit at work. Trust me, I try. The other day I tried to expense three jockstraps and two bottles of poppers but was caught red-handed because I stupidly wrote "Andrew Christian" instead of "United Airlines" in the description.

Let's impeach Donald Trump!

And speaking of "peach," I need an eggplant in mine.

## SEPTEMBER 11

*Dear Diary:*

Today is 9/11. I wonder what would've happened had that fourth plane hit the Whore House (I mean, the White House).

I watched a documentary about the White House the other day. I learned it was gut-renovated from the inside and is no longer the house it used to. What a shame.

When I was a young gay man, I remember hanging out with George Washington at the White House. We ordered hookers and drank beer. Nothing has changed and the hookers are still there. Only now we don't call them hookers: we call them Melania and Ivanka.

Back in the day, everyone was welcome inside the White House. You could walk in and say, "Hamilton, you and me—outside! For a duel!"

And now? You create a plastic replica of the president's head *as a joke*, douse it in ketchup, and ruin your career. Right, Kathy Griffin? Yes, the president should be the most protected person because we cannot make executive decisions without him. It was true for Barack Obama. ISIS, racists, and Osama Bin Laden were after him. Who's after Donald Trump? Kathy Griffin with a bottle of Heinz?

I remember how in 2009 we went to wars, fought for equality, and the president actually meant something.

Wow, 9/11 makes me so patriotic!

## SEPTEMBER 12

*Dear Diary:*

I've been sleeping so well lately. My favorite sleeping aid is a glass of wine, a martini, ten mg of melatonin, a Benadryl, and a shot of NyQuil. I wanna trademark this cocktail and call it "The Amy Winehouse" with the following slogan: "Sleep like you're dead."

## SEPTEMBER 13

*Dear Diary:*

I used a shoehorn today, and now I'm wondering why it's called a horn? Did I miss something? Does it produce music somehow? Noise? Anything? The only noise the shoehorn makes is against my ass when Carlos spanks me.

## SEPTEMBER 14

*Dear Diary:*

Carlos and I watched *Titanic* last night. That movie gives me the creeps. Are people still surprised the *R.M.S. Titanic* sank? Listen, if you cast someone like Kate Winslet with those humongous knockers, of course it'll sink—and kill Leonardo DiCaprio in the process. Next time cast Janet Jackson, and even if your ship sinks anyway at least you'll get a nipple show out of it.

## SEPTEMBER 15

*Dear Diary:*

I bought guacamole and a large bag of tortilla chips for lunch. The bag had a picture of two overblown tortilla chips the size of a Rottweiler. Underneath "Enlarged to show texture" was written as if anybody (unless you're Jessica Simpson) was unaware the picture was exaggerated.

I know what happened. Some customer has sued the company for misleading information—"I thought this was the real size of the tortilla chips!"—and from now on, the company must spell it out. Like, whose throat would fit a Rottweiler? I don't wanna point fingers, but have you seen the size of Eva Mendes's mouth?

But maybe that's why, during my single days, when a guy asked for my pictures, he also asked for some butthole close-ups, which I never understood at the time. I mean, a butt is a butt and (unless you're Donald Trump) a penis is a penis and not an oyster mushroom.

But now I understand why they wanted my close-ups. Guys don't care what's inside the package. They just wanna see the texture.


## SEPTEMBER 16

*Dear Diary:*

I got paid two weeks ago and, since I no longer have any money left over, I must live on credit for the next two weeks. In case American Express decides to cut me off mid-month, I typically pre-purchase my poppers in advance.

I love my multitasking nature of pre-buying and pre-ordering everything. My rent, utilities, and credit card payments are on auto-pay, while vodka, Gas-X, and Tums are on auto-delivery. If I could pre-suck Carlos a month in advance to save time, I would.

## SEPTEMBER 17

*Dear Diary:*

Today is four months with Carlos! We decided to celebrate by not celebrating, to save money. By that I mean we only ordered one bottle of wine with dinner at an Italian/Ethiopian fusion restaurant—and not three like we typically would.

I have a problem with fusion restaurants because their food literally creates explosions. Italian and Ethiopian fusion was not an exception and was unstable like nuclear fissions. I still feel how lasagna and injera are fusing in my stomach, creating reactions I've only seen in a chemical laboratory. So much for saving money. Now we know: if you want a fusion, you will get what you asked for at a fusion restaurant.

## SEPTEMBER 18

*Dear Diary:*

I've been itchy in my anus and went to see a dermatologist. The doctor examined me and concluded it was psoriasis caused by stress.

She asked, "What kind of problems can you possibly have, a young gay man? Why are you stressed?"

I said, "Listen, judgy Hunchback. I have lots of problems! I'm broke and can't afford organic produce, Amazon delayed my poppers this month, and the last time I blew Carlos I spent all day at work with a pube sticking out of my mouth, and nobody—including Hung—told me! That's why I'm stressed and itchy all over the place. I need oxy to feel better."

"You're not getting oxy," she said, "but here's some anti-itching cream. Apply it twice daily—don't forget."

"I won't," I said. "I'll just set a reminder next to my twice-a-day douching."

## SEPTEMBER 19

*Dear Diary:*

After searching for jobs all afternoon, I texted Bagwis to complain: *"Ugh, I hate every posting!"*

Bagwis replied: *"White privilege. Most of us don't get choices like you, skinny whore!"*

I got offended at first, but I know that white privilege is a problem.

When I immigrated in 2007 I couldn't find a job with my given Soviet name: Dazdraperma Ivanovich Preobrazhensky. One HR lady even replied back with: "Honey, if you want a job in the United States, change your fucking name."

So I did, and as soon as I did offer letters started flying in from left and right. Do you think that was a coincidence? My potential employers wouldn't give me a chance (whether I was white or not) because I was *absolutely* an immigrant with my Soviet name, and now finding a job is never a problem.

Unfortunately, employers only care that I'm white and American. Nobody cares about my other talents anymore. I can deadlift fifty pounds, I can shop with my voice with the Amazon Alexa app, and I can give you a prostate massage with my tongue.

## SEPTEMBER 20

*Dear Diary:*

I hate my boss because he fat-shamed me again! He took me aside today and said, "There's only enough room for one chunky thing at the office—and it's called *salsa!*"

## SEPTEMBER 21

*Dear Diary:*

Carlos texted me asking whether I wanted to attend a pup play. I don't know how to react. A pup play is a sexual expression when gay men dress up and pretend to act like dogs.

I mean . . . I've done my share of pup play in the form of doggy style. Is that what Carlos wants? Since we've only been dating for four months, I don't wanna ask Carlos to be more transparent or he'll think I'm a complete moron.

That's something he should find out on his own.

## SEPTEMBER 22

*Dear Diary:*

Carlos made a mistake! He meant to invite me to a *puppy* play, and I looooove puppies! I'm not sure exactly where we're going, but Carlos is rich so maybe he's taking me to England, and I looooove London! Can't wait to have my penis back to eighteen.

Or maybe we're dog-sitting for a friend of his! Either way I'm down. I have a trustworthy face and friends trust me with their pooches way too often, which is a shame. One (former) friend learned this lesson the hard way: his dog escaped on my watch (oopsies), which was when my phone number magically changed overnight and I moved two hundred miles away to avoid getting murdered.

## SEPTEMBER 23

*Dear Diary:*

So, the other day when Carlos invited me to a puppy play he was stuck in the Lincoln Tunnel. Because there was no reception, his autocorrect was all over the place, and he actually meant to invite me to a *puppet* play in two days (not pup and not puppy).

I'm gay and I love puppets and the Muppets!

**SEPTEMBER 24**

*Dear Diary:*

Today Carlos came over holding two Broadway tickets to see *Harry Potter and the Cursed Child* in October. He thought the tickets would make me happy.

"Aren't you so excited?" he asked while he was on top of me.

I said, "I've never even seen the movies."

He paused, sat by my side, and said, "That's so fucked up. Why the fuck not?"

I said, "I hate British movies. I once watched a porn clip and couldn't understand a single word said!"

"We watched it together and the guy was gagged."

"Carlos, that's not the point. I heard *Harry Potter* is all about 'magic' or whatever, and the last time I had a hand inside my butt magically disappear was far from magical—it was a disaster."


**SEPTEMBER 25**

*Dear Diary:*

The puppet show starring Carlo's friend Abhimanyu was phenomenal, and it was called *Hand to God*. In Spanish, it's *Hand to Diaz*, which, I assume, would translate to a show about Cameron Diaz. What happened to that bitch, by the way? Did she die and become an actual angel? She was my favorite actress and nobody can substitute her. That's why I'm back to watching porn exclusively.

Anyhow, nobody discusses that Abhimanyu fists the puppet for two hours and the puppet never even mentions whether the hand inside of him hurts his butt. But that's the name of the play—*Hand to God*—and how fisting—not fasting—is a path to enlightenment.

I love how open the show's producers are about their sexual desires for everyone to watch publicly. After all, voyeurism is my favorite porn!

## SEPTEMBER 26

*Dear Diary:*

Note to self: Never go to Food Bazaar International on an empty stomach. Big fucking mistake! It's similar to being horny and going on Grindr—everyone suddenly looks cute! And while we're at it, it's the same as wanting meth and being Mama June. You just can't help yourself!

## SEPTEMBER 27

*Dear Diary:*

I woke up feeling like death and called a doctor in Oregon to see if it was terminal and whether I could legally kill myself.

The doctor said, "It's just a common cold."

I said. "Ugh—you're no help. Can I at least have some oxy?"

He said, "No, but suck on some Halls."

I said, "If I have to suck on something, Halls is the last thing I'd insert in my mouth!"

The doctor hung up.

Did you know that Oregon is the only state where suicide is legal? First of all, I'm surprised suicide is illegal. They what, put you in prison after saving you?

In the Bible, suicide is an unpardonable sin. Other unpardonable sins are pride, greed, wrath, envy, lust, gluttony, and sloth. So *everything* I love.

From now on, I'm never reading the Bible, and if I want someone to judge me I'll just speak to my boss at work.

**SEPTEMBER 28**

*Dear Diary:*

I heard that death-row inmates can now choose a different form of execution aside from the electric chair. They can choose to take a cocktail of three drugs that will kill them. Only in my days we didn't call it a cocktail, we called it "pulling a Marilyn."

Frankly, do we need a humane way to kill a serial murderer who strangled fifty, drowned sixty, and had sex with eighty? After all that, he cut them up and ate them.

I say fuck serial killers. Listen, bitch, if you wanna be treated humanely, insert your steak knife into a steak and not Annie's throat.

I hate prisons, though. Prison cells remind me of New York City apartments with similar square footage. The authorities are shutting down Rikers Island because the prisoners realized they could pay three thousand dollars a month for the same space, so now they're all moving to other parts of Queens.

## SEPTEMBER 29

*Dear Diary:*

I'm still mad about prisons and death-row inmates. Death-row inmates don't have any fucking imagination. What's up with boring last meal requests? Bagel with lox is everywhere.

Do you know what Steven Woods ordered for his last meal? Two pounds of bacon, a large pizza, fried chicken, hamburgers, fries, garlic bread, and lots of soft drinks—a year of food for a gay man. Or what you'd call Mama June's lunch.

Dennis Bagwell, Robert Dale Conklin, and Robert Alton Harris all got similar items: bacon and hamburgers. That's not a last meal but a menu at McDonald's and also so unhealthy! Not once have any of them ordered hearty oatmeal or an avocado toast on whole wheat. Are they all just animals or what?

Listen, Cannibal Danny, if you want an excellent last meal, order angel's hair with red-eye gravy, and for dessert, order ladyfingers. Make sure the ladyfingers are manicured and cut off before serving. So classy... French!

## SEPTEMBER 30

*Dear Diary:*

Do you know what kind of food I refuse to eat? Food that resembles body parts.

A walnut is shaped like a brain (and is literally the size of Tila Tequila's brain) and why would anyone eat sweet potatoes when they resemble a stomach?

If I were gonna eat myself, I'd start with my butt. It's nice and juicy and (Carlos has told me many times) delicious. But to eat a stomach? No, thanks, a stomach is too acidic, my heart is too sweet, and my blood is too alkaline.

No, no, and no. I graduated from culinary school, so I'm classy and enjoy eating balanced meals. Listen, when I suck a dick there better be a facial, and when I eat dinner it better be light—so I don't have to barf for too long.

# OCTOBER

#TBT. I was once Cleopatra for Halloween. I look like a hooker because I wore a slutty Cleopatra costume—commando.

## OCTOBER 1

*Dear Diary:*

Today during the massage, I asked Jessica to be gentle on me.

She said, "Gentle? Massage must be hard. You want the knots out."

"No, Jessica, *you* want the knots out. I want a gentle massage today."

"Then it's not a massage but an exfoliation!"

"Then fucking exfoliate me!"

She left the room and came back with a Roomba and a mop.

## OCTOBER 2

*Dear Diary:*

Went to dinner with Bagwis at a sketchy Chinese restaurant in Woodside. The awning had a sign: "The best Chinese food in the Tri-State area!"

Wouldn't the best Chinese food be in China? Or at least in Flushing, Queens? When you have a Russian Pofistal on the grill, a Jamaican Teetus on the dishes, and a Korean chef Jae-suk on the sauté station, that's not the best Chinese food. That's a Broadway show called *Waitress*.

My pork fried rice tasted meh and I don't get it. You don't need any skills to burn rice on high heat. You can do it with one eye closed. In fact, you can even do it blindfolded with a traffic cone up your butt. Trust me, I know what I'm talking about.

Burning rice is easy.

I'm getting disappointed in New York's restaurant life. Just because I can't afford a Michelin star restaurant, there's no reason I should eat mediocre food. When you smash something green against a plate and serve it, that's not guacamole, that's the fucking Grinch.

## OCTOBER 3

*Dear Diary:*

I hate even thinking about going to work.

I might murder somebody today—*if* they're lucky. Murdering is easy! I'm so angry I might torture them until they kill *themselves*. Trust me, I can pull off a mean Ted Bundy, or I'll lock them in a fucking basement like Joe Goldberg from *You*.

I called out since my anger is out of control, which means everyone is lucky to stay alive today. Don't tell me being me doesn't save lives! I'm saving turtles by using reusable straws, children by fasting, and now New Yorkers by staying home.

## OCTOBER 4

*Dear Diary:*

I watched *The Great British Bake Off* and realized that because I'm so gay I'm like a beignet. We both get stuffed, we're sweet, and people wanna eat us until they're blue in the face.

**OCTOBER 5**

*Dear Diary:*

Carlos took me to watch his favorite Broadway show, *Come from Away*. It wasn't about Emma Watson, Penélope Cruz, or other immigrants from oversees.

*Come from Away* is based on a true story: on September 11, 2001, the Federal Aviation Administration prohibited airplanes from flying over the U.S., and all the flights detoured to a small town in Canada called Gander.

I'm always cautious when people say a story is true. When I call out it's also a "true story," if you catch my drift. I even lock my phone with the same passcode as Kanye West: 0000. That's also a "true story."

But since *Come from Away* is Carlos's favorite show, I don't want him to read my diary one day and feel like I was ungrateful—he paid for the tickets! So if anyone asks: I fucking loved the show and never gave Carlos a quick blow job in the bathroom at the intermission.

True story!


**OCTOBER 6**

*Dear Diary:*

I went pumpkin picking somewhere on Long Island with Carlos and two friends. I hate traveling past Throggs Neck, so it was torture to sit in a bumpy truck for two hours. I'm OCD and get bored quickly. Plus, Carlos and I woke up late and had no time for coffee, so my resting bitch face upstaged Anna Wintour. I survive on coffee the way Wilt Chamberlain survives on pussy and I drink it faster than Trump tweets. I have my coffee the way Larry King gets married and divorced: as soon as I wake up and often throughout the day.

Pumpkin picking was fun, though. There was more orange all over the place than in the Coxsackie Correctional Facility, and I would know—my ex is staying there.

I picked a giant pumpkin and carved it into a hurricane. The design looked scary and aggressive, unstable, and unpredictable, with a bad haircut, and a lust for killing.

My friends said the pumpkin looked like Kim Jong-un.

**OCTOBER 7**

*Dear Diary:*

Ever since Carlos invited me to see *Harry Potter and the Cursed Child* on Broadway, he's also made me watch *all* the movies. The movies were long and tedious, and I became Slytherin on the couch and Gryffindor in my pouch.

If you don't know what that means, then watch the fucking movies. There are only five million of them.

**OCTOBER 8**

*Dear Diary:*

I love that I'm gay. Gay men eliminate problems from the very beginning and avoid any miscommunication.

For instance, we don't call it "cheating"; we call it an "open relationship."

We also don't call them "drugs"; we call them "poppers."

And we certainly don't call the airline for poor people "Spirit Airlines"; we call it "urinal with wings."

## OCTOBER 9

*Dear Diary:*

I've been thinking about some boring brand names (like Spirit Airlines) that I could fabulously revamp.

Why call something Microsoft? Call it Micro*hard*—that's how we gays like it. Or why call something Apple when apples have calories and sugar? Plus, you have to peel them first. When I come over for a hookup, all your clothes better be peeled off beforehand.

And last, why call something after your ex, like FedEx? If you wanna call anything after your ex, just call it Asshole.

## OCTOBER 10

*Dear Diary:*

Carlos took me to see *Harry Potter and the Cursed Child* (Part I) on Broadway. It was forty hours long and we're seeing Part II tomorrow.

Good night. I'm too exhausted to write another wor

## OCTOBER 11

*Dear Diary:*

*Harry Potter and the Cursed Child* (Part II) was incredible! I loved the magic and hot actors, but if we made it gay the show would be even more popular.

We would call the show *Harry Otter*. The otter is not as chubby and hairy as a bear, but not as rawboned and smooth as a twink.

*Harry Otter* is about me, a simple boy from Astoria who (in Part I) grows up to become a magician. His tricks include: making anal beads disappear, dick-swallowing, and dry douching.

In Part II, we learn more about dry douching, dry humping, and dry spells. Harry turns twinks into otters, bears into gym rats, and ugly ducklings into hunks. Harry likes black magic and "parTy" drugs, and he can make snow appear and disappear—all with just one nostril—akin to Robert Downey Jr. and Mama June.

The show ends with an orgy just like in *Caligula*, and the audience can participate if they buy a jockstrap from the gift shop beforehand.

## OCTOBER 12

*Dear Diary:*

Drove to Bear Mountain today for some leaf-peeping with Carlos and his family.

It was gorgeous everywhere you looked. I looked out the window and it was picturesque, and when I looked in the rearview mirror my reflection was beautiful. After a facial the previous night I looked amazing!

Bear Mountain, however, was a disappointment. If you name something Bear Mountain you better bring some fucking bears, or at least hire some cute guys to walk around *bare*.

We drove for two hours but I didn't see a single animal, which is a shame because I was looking forward to meeting Jocelyn Wildenstein.

For dinner, we had Ecuadorian food in Peekskill. Do you know what Jocelyn Wildenstein had for dinner? Regrets.

## OCTOBER 13

*Dear Diary:*

Spent an evening with Bagwis and we went to see a drag show in Queens. I love queens, Queens, and drag. We have more drag queens in Queens than there are letters in Mississippi.

And speaking of that trashy state, I once read that when Bloomberg restricted portion sizes to prevent obesity in New York, Mississippi Governor Phil Bryant—to make fun of us—signed a law that prevented limiting drink and portion sizes, so now you can double, triple, or quadruple anything in Mississippi.

Dr. Phil moved there immediately.

I also don't understand why police officers ask you to spell Mississippi during a drunk test. What's there to spell? If I really wanna spell Mississippi, I'll just say, "Dump."

Have you been to Jackson? There are a hundred and sixteen thousand people and only two teeth among them. I'd appreciate

Mississippi more if they changed their name to Missippissi, Missigreasi, or Sissikissi. Because that's funny.

There are only three things I like about Mississippi: One, the Homochitto National Forest—because I love everything with the word "homo" attached to it. Two, the fact Mississippi is far away from New York. And three, reread the number two.

## OCTOBER 14

*Dear Diary:*

Today is Columbus Day and everybody is celebrating. What's there to celebrate? Have you been to Columbus Circle or Columbus, Ohio? Honey Boo Boo boring.

If you wanna make something fabulous don't call it after Columbus. Buy a boa, dip it in glitter, and attach the word "homo" at the end (read my last entry about the Homochitto National Forest).

Instead of saying, "Columbus Circle," you could say: "Columbus Homo Circle." Do you see how much more intelligent that reads?

Or you could say, "There's a new bush in Homo Triangle. The bush is nicely trimmed and smells like Old Spice, timber with sandalwood."

You could also say, "Hundreds of seamen are protesting in Homo Square. People give oral speeches and I wonder whether there's an orgy or a rally. Police horsemen are all over the place. Only they're not horse*men*, they're horse*men*."

# OCTOBER 15

*Dear Diary:*

I finally decided to get another roommate because I'm tired of being broke. I was reluctant after living with Anna from Louisiana but figured that maybe things would work out better if I lived with a boy.

I tried ordering a male roommate from Amazon.com, but couldn't find ones made in the U.S. and not China, so I looked on RoommatesWhoDontKill.com, a sister site of RoommatesWhoKill.com. I have nothing against items or people assembled in China, but, similar to produce and boyfriends, I like to keep it local.

In the meantime, I had to remodel my apartment. I donated my old furniture to the dump downstairs, also known as my neighbor, Juan. In exchange for a review on the IMDB, my friend Lindsay Lohan stole some paint from the Home Depot for me, so I painted my kitchen and bathroom in fifty shades of gay: blue, green, and fabulous.

Everything looks incredible now. Since I didn't get any responses from any trustworthy websites I posted an ad on Facebook. A friend of my ex-boyfriend's ex—who's a friend of a former college roommate's friend's hookup and knows someone from prison—wants to come over to see the apartment tomorrow.

I'm happy to know we aren't strangers and basically family!

## OCTOBER 16

*Dear Diary:*

My newly painted kitchen and bathroom look fantastic! Also, a potential roommate came over, a twenty-year-old twink from Italy. His name is Geppetto and he's lived in New York for a year. We hit it off right away because he knew exactly what gifts to bring: two bottles of vodka and three bottles of poppers.

We skipped the small gay talk about barfing, celebrities, or why tops—like dinosaurs—are extinct from Astoria. Instead, we confabulated about douching—my favorite topic—and Geppetto paid me a deposit afterward.

## OCTOBER 17

*Dear Diary:*

Today is my five-month anniversary with Carlos and we decided to stay home and cook for each other. It was his idea.

Carlos said, "Let's stay home and cook for each other." After that, he sat down on the couch, leaving me in the kitchen with three pounds of bottom round steak.

For "each other" meant I had to cook for *"him,"* which took me three hours.

When I returned home to Astoria later that evening, tired and annoyed, I said, "Alexa, add Carlos to my shit list."

Alexa said, "I already have, right after he ordered bottom round steak for your anniversary dinner. I thought he was rich. Can't he afford Wagyu beef?"

"Alexa, it was bottom round. As long as there's the word 'bottom' involved, he goes for it."

**OCTOBER 18**

*Dear Diary:*

My Spanish is going well, so I started taking Japanese too just to spice things up. I'm good at Japanese because the Japanese can't stop bowing, and I bow my head at least four times a week.

**OCTOBER 19**

*Dear Diary:*

I'm learning my first Japanese words, starting with the numerals, and Japanese people, I realized, are just like me because they love multitasking!

*Ju* means ten, *ju* means Jew, and Jew also means every movie starring Jesse Eisenberg.

*Yon* means four, *yon* means yawn, and yawn also means my reaction to the movie *Hot Pursuit*.

Six is *roku*, which is also a streaming device.

*Sun* is three, and *ni* is two, so if I wanna say my age in Japanese (thirty-two), I can say I'm yellow and *sunni* like the sun.

**OCTOBER 20**

*Dear Diary:*

I want another job so bad, but what are my credentials? I was born in a country that no longer exists—the USSR. Is there even proof it ever existed? Then I immigrated to the United States in

2007, received political asylum in 2009, and changed my name. How sketchy is that?

I went to college in 2005, and, upon graduating, the college closed its doors for good as if it had never existed. Then I went to Natural Gourmet Institute and it closed the very next year in 2018. After meeting my first boyfriend at a bar in Astoria called Mixx, the bar went out of business in 2011 and my boyfriend died under mysterious circumstances...

Everything in my life disappears! Boyfriends mysteriously die, schools close, and when I lived alone even the food from my fridge disappeared as well—and I don't eat!

Everything I attend shuts down.

The only reason I never applied to Harvard is not that I'm poor or inadequate or whatever. It's because I'm selfless and if I went it would close down. I wanna make sure American children have access to decent education. I'm just like Mother Teresa: do the missionary, travel, and refuse banquets. Also, how many turtles did I save this year alone?

Anywhere I go I seem to wreak havoc and close every damn thing...

Unless we're talking about my legs. Those babies always stay open.

## OCTOBER 21

*Dear Diary:*

Studied more Spanish today, or should I say S-PUNISH? Because it *feels* like punishment. I'm reading a book called *Cincuenta Shades of Gray*, some sort guide on how to tie rope, and I need to brush up on my knot-making abilities for a fantasy of mine.

To show off my new language skills, I texted my boss in Spanish the way Carlos taught me: *"Chupame, puta,"* which, Carlos said means "Hi, I'm running late."

## OCTOBER 22

*Dear Diary:*

I just saw this sign on a building on Thirtieth Avenue and I'm appalled. The sign said: NO BALL PLAYING.

So rude and misandrist. Have you ever been a gay man? I'm sorry, but sometimes we just can't help it and must play with our balls! We're basically cats. Don't worry, I reported those bitches to the Department of Buildings for their stupid signs.

## OCTOBER 23

*Dear Diary:*

Today is Carlos's mom's birthday (her name is Maria) and we went to a whole new world called New Jersey. People say New Jersey smells and I disagree. It reeks! I had to pull out my nipple clamps and stick them over my nose.

Maria is so selfless and wanted no presents, so I listened and purchased none (like a good boy), but Carlos, unbeknownst to me, brought Maria a gift anyhow—a cleaning robot—and made me look cheap. Material things don't matter. From Oprah to the Dalai Lama to Mama June, everyone says the same: "On your death bed, you'll only remember experiences—like being rich, being spiritual, or being on meth—no cleaning robots in sight."

## OCTOBER 24

*Dear Diary:*

Note to self: after making a big deal about "experiences" the night before, apologize to Carlos for calling him a bitch. After all, it's not his fault he's not spiritual like Oprah, the Dalai Lama, or Mama June. He's young and has so much to learn, so you must remain patient. Remember, it will all pay off once you marry him—*then* make him pay for everything.

Until then, apologize.


## OCTOBER 25

*Dear Diary:*

What kind of experiences can Carlos and I have before 2019 ends? We've seen every drag show, we've dined in every restaurant, and we've visited every glory hole. Now what?


## OCTOBER 26

*Dear Diary:*

After work, I was feeling lethargic and needed a pick-me-up. I said, "Alexa, tell me a joke."

Alexa said, "OK. Why couldn't Mama June cross to the other side?"

"Why?"

"She didn't smoke enough meth."

## OCTOBER 27

*Dear Diary:*

Cleaned my apartment for hours. My roommate Geppetto is moving in tomorrow and I must guarantee no trace of Anna from Louisiana can be found anywhere.

In Spanish, her name is Locas from Secaucus.

Anyway, enough about her! Not another word. I don't want any reminders of that Charisma, Uniqueness, Nerve, and Talent—

—or, if you abbreviate it: CUNT.


## OCTOBER 28

*Dear Diary:*

Geppetto moved in today and said, "What forms of payment do you accept?"

I said, "I take cash, Venmo, checks, stocks in Apple, 401(k), government bonds, wire transfers, gold slips, and even equities in your escort business."

You can tell I'm desperate for cash.

Geppetto said, "You're like Fire Island: anything goes."

I said, "You have no fucking idea, Geppetto."

He said, "We are now officially best friends."

## OCTOBER 29

*Dear Diary:*

Went to dinner with my coworker Hung in the Village. Hung has an unfortunate last name, by the way: Taylor. I know, I know, it sounds just like mine, but I believe Taylors are unfortunate.

Take Elizabeth Taylor, for example. She married and divorced eight times, and then what happened to her? She died.

Zachary Taylor, our twelfth president, also died. Well, he's technically alive, but because he's a seventy-year-old gay man, it means he's basically dead due to the ageism.

And that's it, no more famous Taylors!

OK, there's obviously one other Taylor . . . but I don't wanna be associated with someone whose last name describes the way I get on my knees: Swift.

## OCTOBER 30

*Dear Diary:*

I'm trying to send postcards to every hookup from my past with: "I have a boyfriend now, bitch!" I want the whole world to know!

I needed stamps, so I ordered fifty Forever Stamps from the USPS website and they charged me five dollars for shipping.

Are they fucking serious? The stamps are *their* product, delivered by *them*, on *their* trucks. It would be cheaper for me to deliver the postcards myself. I'm literally buying shipping *labels*, so why am I paying for getting shipping labels *shipped*?

So dumb!

Not once while at a restaurant has a waiter told me, "Hey, Russian asswipe with a bad haircut. On top of paying for food, you must also pay for plates."

Ridiculous.

When I take the subway, I don't position myself behind the N Train and push it, and when I go for a checkup, I don't touch my own balls for cancer screening.

Some things must come with the package, and those things are shipping tape, shipping labels, and pubic hair.

**OCTOBER 31**

*Dear Diary:*

Happy Halloween! Today, straight people will *dress* like someone else, and gay men will *undress* someone else.

I love the concept of Halloween: going door to door and begging for candy.

A bunch of kids knocked on my door and yelled, "Trick or treat!"

In the gay world it's, "Top or bottom!"

And in Mama June's world it's, "Coke or meth!"

I'm a skinny bitch and don't keep any candy at my place to avoid gaining weight, so since I couldn't treat the kids I had to trick them. I evoked Mother Teresa and told them three great tricks:

1. Listen to what your divorced parents tell you and then do the opposite.

2. You can save on Forever Stamps by stealing them from your office.

3. Unless your goal is to shit for a week, don't order lamb from the food cart on the corner of Broadway and Thirty-sixth Street.

# NOVEMBER

Harry Potter and the Cursed Child. I think the ugly, I mean cursed child is Honey Boo Boo, BTW.

## NOVEMBER 1

*Dear Diary:*

Wine is so pretentious! I just purchased a bottle of Italian Chianti, and on the label, a gastronomic suggestion was printed: "This Chianti is great with fish, meats, poultry, vegetables, and mature Italian cheeses."

Got it. So it goes with everything. What kind of a tip is that? If you're giving suggestions, be specific! Like: "After two bottles of this Chianti, your mouth will open and you'll drop to your knees." I'm just sharing my experience, but yours may be different!

I've had wine for years so I know it goes well with *everything*. Your gastronomic suggestion is unwelcome and unnecessary.

Below the "gastronomic suggestion" there was a serving suggestion: "Serve Chianti at room temperature of sixty-eight degrees."

I hope they're joking. When was the last time you went to a bar, and upon getting a Cabernet, you stuck a thermometer in the glass? What would you even say? "Yo, jackass. My Cabernet is eighty-six degrees. Cool it the fuck down!"

Do you know what the bartender would say? "No, jackass. *You* cool the fuck down. *You're* eighty-sixed."

## NOVEMBER 2

*Dear Diary:*

Do you know what is more pretentious than wine? Whiskey. Other alcoholic drinks you drink, but whiskey? It must be consumed in three distinct ways: neat, on the rocks, or mixed in a cocktail. So pretentious!

Whiskey connoisseurs purchase special whiskey rocks and whiskey stones, and what do we, vodka drinkers, have? Kidney stones. Or is it just me?

And besides, I hate Jack Daniel's. It's nothing personal. "Jack" is my landlady's last name and I hate that I'm paying the numbskull a fortune and "Daniel's" is a possessive, and possessives ruin every sentence!

PS. I also hate Macy's, Reese's Pieces, and Lay's for exactly the same reason.

## NOVEMBER 3

*Dear Diary:*

My precious fish Kiki died because I've been so neglectful of her. If you wanna blame anyone, blame Carlos. I'm seldom home, enjoying my newly-purchased traffic cone at Carlos's, so Kiki must have died from hunger.

Rest in peace, my special baby (or, as Daddy used to call you, Dumb Bitch).

## NOVEMBER 4

*Dear Diary:*

Carlos and I went to New Jersey to visit his mom, Maria. After dinner, we borrowed Maria's car to meet my weed dealer in Ho-Ho-Kus as I was out of Gorilla Glue #4.

When we stopped for gas, I noticed a warning sign at the station. "NJ State law: it is illegal to service yourself."

What was that sign about? Are people in New Jersey so lazy that they can't get out of the car and pump their own gas?

Upon thinking further about it, I realized it makes sense. When you're at a restaurant, you don't barge into the kitchen, yelling, "Ramsay, I'll have the crab cakes," after which you serve them yourself. No, you have servers to help you along. And then you have laxatives to help you move your bowels along.

In the evening, when Carlos and I went to a watering hole called the Ho-Ho-Kus Eagle, it turned out to be a sex party for bears. The bears were all servicing each other because in New Jersey you can't service yourself.


## NOVEMBER 5

*Dear Diary:*

Took a work client, Will, for sushi and to kiss his ass. Will is a little slow and half the time he's *Will Not*. I let him choose the place (to make him feel like he's in command) and Will Not picked the worst Japanese restaurant in Manhattan: Jackie Chan.

I told the waiter, "But Jackie Chan is Chinese, not Japanese."

He said, embarrassed, "I know, quite ironic, isn't it?"

The food was also ironic. Every menu item was named after a celebrity, which I found beyond dumb: EdaMama June, Raw Tuna Turner, Mike Pad Thaison, TerryYaki Crews, Dax Shephard "Soba" Noodles, Paris Hilton's Crabs, the Queen Latifah roll, etc.

After eating the Queen Latifah roll, Will and I started talking about the movie *The Secret Life of Bees*. Will told me bees are disappearing worldwide faster than money from my checking account. Here I was, saving penguins (or was it turtles?) while bees were in danger. When bees disappear and nobody can pollinate flowers, we'll all die.

Great. So now what? On top of drinking through reusable straws and using tote bags instead of plastic barf bags, I also have to avoid honey?

Caring about the environment is exhausting. Can I get a fucking break?

**NOVEMBER 6**

*Dear Diary:*

Note to self: stop blaming yourself. Blame Anna from Louisiana. Turtles die because she doesn't recycle, eggplants die because she eats vegan, and bees die because she doesn't douche. Douching releases nutrients like nitrogen, phosphorus, and potassium to the soil, helping plants grow and allowing bees to collect pollen.

Being gay helps everyone!

## NOVEMBER 7

*Dear Diary:*

I realized I have zero straight friends outside of Facebook, on which I have a ton of straight friends from all over the world (and even Bessemer, Alabama).

Long, long ago, when I was in my early twenties, France gifted us the Statue of Liberty and it was such a beautiful ceremony! I wish Carlos had been there. Amazon had certified the shipping, and even if France didn't accept returns, the statue was delivered to New York in two days from China.

Sorry, I got distracted.

So, straight friends...

I meant to say the following: in my early twenties, my friends were mainly straight girls, or "catamite termagants" as we called them in the good old days. These days we call them "fag hags." All my catamite termagants are now married and homebound (some are literally tied up in bed), and some even have kids (or "neonates," as we called them in 1886).

I miss the past. I miss the roaring twenties, hippies, and even communism. Why communism? Because we shared stuff, and sharing is caring. We're blinded by consumerism these days! Like, do I really need to purchase five non-recyclable silicone dildos when I could borrow my roommate's?

## NOVEMBER 8

*Dear Diary:*

Hacking has changed everything when it comes to celebrities. The latest scandal involved Jennifer Lawrence, when someone hacked into her iCloud account and started selling her nudes. I've been trying to sell mine for years on Times Square but nobody cares! I even posted my iCloud password on Grindr—bottom29—but nobody's interested. Well, the joke's on them because I'm not twenty-nine but thirty-two, bitch! Ha!

## NOVEMBER 9

*Dear Diary:*

Hosted a housewarming party for my new roommate, Geppetto.

Geppetto told me he liked to play with wood, so I gave him a saw as a present. And then later, if he decides to saw his boyfriend in half, he doesn't need to look further than his mattress, under which Geppetto keeps the saw. Plus, we have plenty of space in the freezer next to Tito's.

## NOVEMBER 10

*Dear Diary:*

Trump and his Ukraine call are all over the news. People are now serious about impeachment, which is highly unlikely.

The first president to get impeached was Andrew Johnson, a Democrat from Tennessee. He was impeached because he wasn't classy, but have you been to Tennessee? Nashville is OK, but Andrew Johnson was from Elizabethton and was removed from office for thinking it's spelled "Elizabeth's thong." What a shame.

Then we had Nixon, a Republican, who resigned before being impeached, like a sissy boy. On the contrary, after getting impeached, Bill Clinton served the rest of his second term as if nothing happened. Do you know what I call that? Class.

Getting impeached is like farting in a crowded elevator—it's embarrassing. Nixon exited on the first floor, but Clinton stayed, farted, and said, "Did anyone else have Hillary's beignets last night at the Correspondents' Dinner? I think I'm lactose-intolerant. Boy, do my eyes sting. Beignets can make you quite gassy, can't they?"

And then he exited the elevator when his term was up.

## NOVEMBER 11

*Dear Diary:*

Went to a gala today with Carlos. The charity was about saving dolphins or adopting orphans, I'm not sure which. If you want me to care—fucking speak louder! After an extensive five-course menu I'm bloated, and that's the price I'm willing to pay.

Why does it take forever and a half to adopt? By the time you manage, the child you're trying to adopt is already fifty-six and seeking to adopt *you* from a geriatric facility in Florida.

Even if you adopt faster than Meryl Streep collects Oscars, you still have to pay two hundred thousand dollars per child. Do you call that affordable? That's the price of the Somalia's debt.

If you wanna have a fun gala, host a gala for gay men. Just don't call it a "gala"; call it an "orgy."

## NOVEMBER 12

*Dear Diary:*

Winter is finally here. Yesterday, my shlong felt so cold, he refused to come out. I don't understand how something so big (he said modestly) can shrink. Have you ever seen the Empire State Building lose a few floors when the temperature drops to thirty degrees outside? No, right? I've seen Mama June lose a few teeth, but it was hot and humid, and it's a much different story involving crystal meth.

But seriously, though, when your hands are freezing you have gloves, and when your feet are freezing you have someone's mouth to warm them up, but how do you warm Truth? It's not like I could approach a heater at work, stick my shlong out, and say, "Come on, Truth, be a good boy. Come on out and give Daddy a hug."

That would confuse Hung.

Hung would say, "Wait, bro, you have a kid?"

## NOVEMBER 13

*Dear Diary:*

Went to a Friendsgiving. It's when friends get together and eat turkey before Thanksgiving. I always thought Friendsgiving was something else, and for the past nine years I've been Friends-head-giving regularly. I'm a giver through and through, but I like to receive as well and that's what Friendsgiving is all about: you reap what you sow.

I said, "Alexa, what's the definition of the word sow?"

Alexa said, "Sow, verb, means to be thickly covered with or to seed. It also means cause to appear or spread."

So I did what I know best: I've been thickly covered with Carlos' seeds, and I planted a few of my seeds as well. Plus, my legs have spread so much they've become a dip, so come on over to put your baguettes inside me. It's Friendsgiving, after all—the door is open!

## NOVEMBER 14

*Dear Diary:*

My boss is getting on my nerves! He's so needy he resembles a cat, and I'm developing an allergy!

For instance, he told me today, "Your H&M pants look quite wrinkly around the knees. Were you blowing Carlos during lunch?"

He's so rude, right? The pants were from Zara!

## NOVEMBER 15

*Dear Diary:*

I've discovered new snacks at Food Bazaar International: cashew-butter-covered cashews and almond-butter-covered almonds. It's genius to invent a product out of itself, but that kind of narcissism makes me nauseous. People are obsessed with everything double. Double standards, anyone?

Why stop there, then? We already have *Zoolander*—a movie written, directed, and starring Ben Stiller—and *Godzilla: Planet of the Monsters*—a movie written, directed, and starring the cast of *Love Island*.

And what do you call a broke, underpaid, and stressed-out millennial? Me.

## NOVEMBER 16

*Dear Diary:*

I'm wiped—like a roll of toilet paper against Anna from Louisiana's ass. I was at the theater all day with Carlos, watching a show in two parts, three hours each.

Why two parts? Anything double makes me nauseous. (If you don't believe me, check the previous entry for November 15.) My hate has nothing to do with the show itself. I'm unable to negatively speak about the show as sneaky Carlos will read my diary one day and cut off my allowance.

The shows—*Long* and *Longer*—were fine, but I'm OCD and need to walk, clean, or give head. Otherwise, I get antsy.

I was joking about having an allowance—I wish! I'm six years older than Carlos, so whenever we're at a party his friends always wonder why he drags *his* daddy along.

I hate this ageist society. When a celebrity couple is two years apart (with the woman being younger, naturally), the haters say, "She looks just like his daughter." If it could happen to Anna Nicole Smith and Billy Wayne Smith—with their minuscule age difference of three hundred years—it could happen to anyone.

Did you know that Anna Nicole Smith's real name was Vickie Lynn Marshall? I love when a celebrity uses a pseudonym. It means they come from a fucked-up background. They'll either die of drug overdose like Marilyn Monroe (aka, Norma Jeane Mortenson), or they'll pay the officials to get their children into a better school like Rebecca Donaldson-Katsopolis (aka, Lori Loughlin).

Hey, Lori Loughlin ... who's *loughlin* now, bitch?

## NOVEMBER 17

*Dear Diary:*

I just received a notification on the Citizens app: "Lazy Susan got stabbed at a UPS store." That's on Union Square near where I work. Yesterday, somebody got stabbed at Walgreens, and I wasn't surprised then either. It's so busy around here with NYU students, hookers, and the long perpetual line at Trader Joe's—another possessive I hate.

When I tried sending a package last week, the line at UPS was a mile long. Plus, Lazy Susan working behind the counter was so fucking slow and sluggish that I put a tray of party cheeses and prosciutto on her head, and we spun her around like the lazy Susan that she was.

I don't understand customer service in New York. If you need extra help, hire it. This is why everyone is getting stabbed.

But it works the other way around too: Are you listening, stabby Tom? If you have a knife, don't stab lazy Susan and apply to culinary school instead. That's what I did.

**NOVEMBER 18**

*Dear Diary:*

Received another horrible haircut today in Koreatown. My stylist, a young Korean gay man, Ji-hun—the same one who cut my hair in June—had spiky blue hair and pink bellbottoms. You know hairstyling is his passion just by looking at him.

He asked, "What should I do for you, handsome twat?"

"Ji-hun, hun, I want the same haircut as in June—"

He interrupted, "Say no more."

But he misunderstood. Now I look like Mama June.


**NOVEMBER 19**

*Dear Diary:*

I feel better about myself after I saw Hung's haircut. Not the one on his head, though. I saw his bush in the bathroom "by accident" and he's absolutely bald down there! No wonder Hung is single. Who would date a grown straight man with a Brazilian and a willy the size of a cocktail sausage?


**NOVEMBER 20**

*Dear Diary:*

You know what else I don't find attractive on a man, along with bald balls and limp gherkins? Bald legs. If you don't have any leg hair, there's a great invention—pants. Wear them. If you're swimming, fine, but there's no reason you should look like a dolphin on dry land.

## NOVEMBER 21

*Dear Diary:*

Just finished a documentary about Mercury. No, not Freddie Mercury—planet Mercury. Mercury is the smallest planet and has no atmosphere. There are more craters on its surface than plastic in Lil' Kim's knockers.

I'm obsessed with Mercury because Mercury is perfect for cooking and storing food. During the day, the temperature skyrockets to nine hundred degrees and you can cook a whole turkey under an hour. At night, the temperature drops to negative three hundred and you don't need a refrigerator.

The reason why I'm moving to Mercury is not because of its great kitchen (and you know how much I like cooking) but because on Mercury, you weigh less because the force of gravity is different. I'd only weigh fifty-six fucking pounds! I can even return the Peloton bike I purchased in credit because I'll no longer need it!

## NOVEMBER 22

*Dear Diary:*

Attended another Friendsgiving tonight. There's more turkey in me than extensions in Khloé Kardashian's hair. I'm so stuffed I may as well be a teddy bear. In a toy world I'm definitely either a Barbie or a dildo, because I'm skinny and blond like the first, and happy to be anywhere else like the second.

## NOVEMBER 23

*Dear Diary:*

I've been thinking all day about toys. Growing up I had none, because we were underprivileged and lived on food stamps. To make up for a basically "wasted childhood," I started appreciating toys as an adult.

When I was seven, I remember playing with VHS tapes, bobby pins, and pots and pans, because that's all we had. I think it was selfish of my parents to have a baby when they couldn't afford some LEGOs. Look, if I rescued a dog there would be toys and bones everywhere. Even when I had my fish Kiki, a fighting betta fish, Daddy would throw a live goldfish in her tank once in a while—so Kiki could chase and kill it. That's good parenting.

But forget toys, we were also starving—a lot. After my parents' divorce, my mom took care of my brother and me by herself, and she would typically say things like, "Pick one: Dinner or breakfast? On Monday or Saturday?"

I'm grateful for my training because now, when I need to lose weight, starving comes naturally to me. Just like drinking, sucking, and douching.

**NOVEMBER 24**

*Dear Diary:*

Back in my twenties I remember loving Fridays. Fridays were the epitome of happiness. "Yay! Friday is here. Two days of fun!"

Now I say, "Ugh, today is Friday. Monday is in two days."

I hate my job and every day at work is torture, and I know torture. I've sat through all four hours of *Gone with the Wind*.

**NOVEMBER 25**

*Dear Diary:*

"Alexa, when is the season of spreading joy?"

Alexa said, "When there are bells, bells, bells everywhere."

"Sure. Do you know how else you know there's joy? When you enter the Patriots' locker room, and there are balls, balls, balls everywhere."

**NOVEMBER 26**

*Dear Diary:*

My coworker Hung asked me whether I ever wanted to be straight.

I said, "Yes, once. I wanted to have a girlfriend named Joy, and when somebody like you asked me what I was doing, I'd say, 'I'm spreading Joy!'"

## NOVEMBER 27

*Dear Diary:*

I was spreading joy all day, but subtly (with compliments and kind gestures).

For instance, I told Hung he had a great ass but that I couldn't see it because of his baggy pants, I gave up my seat on the subway once the train got to my stop, and when my boss talked, I actually listened.

He was saying, "Blah, blah, blah."

## NOVEMBER 28

*Dear Diary:*

Today is Thanksgiving, and I'm thankful for so many things. I have all my limbs, all my holes, and a job—even if I hate it. I'm an optimist and I always try to find the silver lining.

The silver lining today is that I'm not Henry Lee Lucas, the guy who confessed to six hundred murders and was fond of having sex with or in front of animals. Listen, if I wanna have sex in front of a beast, I'll just masturbate while watching *Godzilla vs. King Ghidorah*.

On a good note, Carlos and I are going on a road trip tomorrow. We've rented a car, and we're traveling to Pennsylvania to see historical sites, then Shenandoah National Park to see some bears, and Waynesboro, Virginia, to see a drag show.

Four days of road head and seedy motels!

**NOVEMBER 29**

*Dear Diary:*
  Today is day one of our road trip.
  First stop: Gettysburg for their "anal" tree lighting ceremony. I would say *"annual* tree lighting ceremony" but that's not what Carlos did to me this morning.
  Gettysburg is more commonly known as a town with more confederate flags per capita than fashion sense, so the best part of Gettysburg was having a pool at the motel. Carlos loves pools, and I love that I don't have to search for a bathroom if I need to pee. We brought wine, cheese, and grapes to the pool, and I was excited for some romantic time. I've been wondering for a while what it's like to suck someone underwater!
  And then a nine-year-old girl showed up and ruined everything. She came with her father, who plopped himself down on a chair and played on his laptop for two hours, leaving his unusually chatty daughter in the pool with us.
  Ugh!!! I mean, I paid sixty-nine dollars for the motel and expected some class. All I wanted was a peaceful night and some underwater action.
  "What's your name?" she yelled out. "My name's Maryanne! I weight three hundred pounds, I'm in fifth grade, and I'm here with my stepfather."
  I said, "Hi, Chatty Cathy. My name's Jeremy."
  "I don't care, bitch! I'm nine years old, so all I wanna do is talk about myself. Did I tell you I'm in fifth grade? Also, that's my stepdad over there! I don't have any front teeth!"
  "I know!" I said. "I said my name was Jeremy."
  "I don't care about your stupid name. Was it Asshole? Just look, I'm swimming!"

## NOVEMBER 30

*Dear Diary:*

There was only one treadmill at the motel's gym and it wasn't working properly. I felt like I was running on an ice rink. I almost somersaulted backward into a weight rack behind me, which could have been beneficial because it would knock me out, and I needed to catch up on my sleep.

Afterward, Carlos and I went to have complimentary (which means full of carbs) breakfast at the motel. I was furious that there were no pancakes left, but then I noticed Chatty Cathy with a medium-size box from Home Depot full of pancakes in front of her. Mystery solved!

Chatty Cathy yelled out, "Mom, look! These are the homos from the pool! Hi, homos!"

I was so embarrassed for her mom because Chatty Cathy had stolen all the pancakes. I took her mom's hand and whispered, "Next time, use a condom."

These days I find it impossible not to offend parents because they take everything personally. "Your child is a dumb asshole" is not an attack on you as a mother. I'm cranky because I'm on vacation and wanna eat in peace, but to be honest, her child really was a dumb asshole.

Carlos and I have discussed having kids together, a boy first. How cute, right? So cute and huge, it's "cuge." I warned you I loved multitasking words.

But Carlos is exceptionally young, and I'm, well, antique (in the gay world), and if we had a child, the boy would call Carlos his Daddy and me his Granddaddy.

Unfair!

I only have one fucking grey hair, and you can't even see it because it's in my pubes!

# DECEMBER

Gettysburg, PA, tree lighting ceremony. I counted three more Confederate flags. In the same window.

## DECEMBER 1

*Dear Diary:*

Carlos and I traveled to Shenandoah National Park and it was spectacular. We saw a bear taking a dump in the woods. A bear! We saw some animals too.

I grew up in a small Siberian village and learned to appreciate and love nature, and the Shenandoah mountains took me straight home. The Skyline Drive takes you up, up, up—a scenic view all along—and at some point we were so high Snoop Dog dialed me and said he was jealous.

If I said I wanted to return anytime soon, though, I'd be lying. I mean, only for so long can trees keep you entertained. If you must stare at lots of wood for fucking hours, go to IKEA. Or better yet, to my bedroom.


## DECEMBER 2

*Dear Diary:*

Next stop, Fredericksburg! We hit the road pretty early but as soon as we started driving, the road, all of a sudden, became foggy. It was like nothing we've seen before. The fog was so dense that it reminded me of smoke, and it was like driving through Bob Marley's lungs. We moved at five miles per hour for the next thirty minutes, afraid we'd get into a fender bender at higher speed. At some point we were driving so slow I thought I was taking the W Train to work and even texted my boss: *"I'm running late."*

He replied: *"Wow. Even on vacation!"*

When we finally made it to Fredericksburg we visited the house where George Washington grew up. George wasn't even home and some lady "manager" with a lisp, Drew Berryless, was in charge. Rude! If you invite people in, *be* there!

Not only that but the tours were already done for the day. If you give tours or blow jobs, actually give them! I don't understand it. I called Drew in advance and she told me they were open. Did I dial my own anus again?

Drew gave us a brochure at least, and I learned that George Washington was named after a bridge in New York, and Abraham Lincoln was named after a tunnel also in New York.

Do you know what else should be called after a tunnel? My butthole.


**DECEMBER 3**

*Dear Diary:*

On the last day of our vacation, Carlos took me to a Korean spa, and even though the spa was unisex, we had our own men-only area with saunas, hot tubs, and plunge pools.

I love unisex places because then everyone is included, but I didn't love the unibrow manager, Jae-ho, who told us we had to walk barefoot everywhere, even in the elevator.

I told him, "Jae-ho, I'm concerned with getting an athlete's foot."

He replied, "Athlete's foot or your *chubby* foot? Get real, bitch!"

**DECEMBER 4**

*Dear Diary:*

I feel insecure about my weight after Jae-ho's snarky comment. Carlos and I came to the spa after a vacation, so discussing my weight or Mama June was the last thing on my mind after gorging on greasy food and Carlos for a week. It's not like I told Jae-ho, "Excuse me, turd-colored uniform, where's the sauna?" I was polite. All I said was, "Are all Korean saunas this trashy, or is it because we're in New Jersey?"


**DECEMBER 5**

*Dear Diary:*

I just finished a documentary about the Chinese one-child policy that was in effect from 1979 to 2015. The woman in the documentary started her story with how she gave birth. She said her child was born seven weeks early and she was unprepared.

*Unprepared?* What the fuck was she doing for the past seven months? If you need seven months to get ready—like me for work—how long do you think it takes her to douche? She's so lazy! Instead of giving a blow job, she wrapped it in Saran wrap and saved it for later.

## DECEMBER 6

*Dear Diary:*

I was invited to an ugly sweater party. I've never attended one before, and I'm not sure where to get an ugly sweater. I like pretty clothes. Bagwis said I could borrow his, but I heard I don't look good in a color turd or XXXL robes. No, thanks!

Eventually, when I asked Alexa to order me an ugly sweater from the internet, she just ordered me a sweater with a picture of Mama June. So frustrating!

Maybe it's not meant to be. After all, I've missed many parties this season: The Republican Party, Million Moms against Ellen party, and a coffee-douching party.

The last one was held at the White House and hundreds of douchebags came to honor President Trump. In the morning, when the sanitation department came to pick up the trash, their truck was so full they had to throw Ivanka Trump back to the curb.

## DECEMBER 7

*Dear Diary:*

Today is Carlos' birthday!

I'm so happy for him! Actually, I'm happier for myself because now our age difference is only five years (until my thirty-third birthday; then we're back to six).

I'm insecure about my age in this ageist society. My plastic surgeon back in January told me why the face sags: gravity weighs it down. One more reason to move to Mercury! Gravity is only good about one thing: over time, your balls end up on the floor, which is excellent for football practice as you'll need plenty of aerobic activity after hitting sixty.

Do you know how to tell you're old? When people offer you a seat on the subway or when your boyfriend turns twenty-seven.

## DECEMBER 8

*Dear Diary:*

I went for my monthly massage with Jessica. We've been together for twelve months, and we're officially in a relationship.

Jessica is perfect! If I ask her to use a hot stone, she goes to the kitchen, boils some water, and puts a kettle on my back. If I ask her to call me dirty names and spank me, she calls me a filthy whore and scissor-strikes my ass *à la hasami zuki*.

Jessica was poking me for an hour, tenderizing me, which was rejuvenating. She didn't say a word about my "holiday weight" and treated me like I was absolutely normal.

At the end of the massage, I said, "Jessica, can I have some water? A cup is fine."

She seemed scared and yelled, "You're a cop???"

I said, "No! A cup!"

That was the last time I saw Jessica. I guess we broke up.

## DECEMBER 9

*Dear Diary:*

After many drinks at a local gay bar, Bagwis and I had dinner at a Japanese restaurant in Astoria. Astoria is colloquially known as "Actoria" and also as "Fifteen minutes away from Manhattan, but don't fucking kid yourself."

Bagwis was offended when I asked the waiter, "Is your name Haruki Murakami?"

The waiter rolled his eyes and said, "Sure."

I said, "I'll have the shark and a Sapporo."

Bagwis said, "How can you possibly *order* that?"

I said, "What's wrong with it?"

He said, "Change your order immediately."

I said, "Fine! Haruki, no Sapporo for me. Make me a martini."

Bagwis was not satisfied either. He said, "No, bitch. You can't eat sharks if you wanna save the animals—or whatever you're saving."

"Either turtles or giraffes, I don't remember."

"Sharks have lots of mercury!"

"Mercury is good. I'm moving there next year."

Bagwis said, "Plus, they're endangered and rare."

I said, "They can't be *that* rare, considering I found one at a shitty restaurant in Astoria."

Haruki said, "I'll give you a minute," and left.

Bagwis said, "It's fine to order a shark in Vietnam because then it's local."

"That's double standards!"

"If you wanna become a better person, you must start with yourself. Eat better."

I said, "Thanks, Oprah."

So I ended up eating a vegan salad, all along thinking of all the penguins I was saving. Or was it turtles? I can't fucking remember.

## DECEMBER 10

*Dear Diary:*

After dinner with Bagwis, I'm contemplating becoming vegan again, so I finished a documentary about veganism. Even Arnold Schwarzenegger put in his two cents. According to the online reviews, the documentary has lots of inconsistencies and wrong facts. That's because a vegan diet is not profitable for the economy, so everyone is trying to fight it. Next, you'll have a meat company making a documentary about meat. Only they won't call it a documentary—they'll just post it on a porn site.

In the documentary, the narrator mentions that the Roman gladiators ate beans and barley. It's a known fact that the gladiators were strong and didn't need meat to build muscle.

But how did the gladiators' diet become known, you ask? Good question. The scientists had dug up gladiators and cut their bones, and from the bone marrow, the scientists learned about the diet. That's pretty cool! My bones must be full of martinis, cotton balls, and Carlos's sperm.

I got inspired by the documentary and tried to figure out what my roommate Geppetto had eaten by the sounds coming out of the bathroom: loud, trashy, and obnoxious.

Did he eat Donald Trump?

## DECEMBER 11

*Dear Diary:*

My phone is so annoying! When Carlos and I visit New Jersey, I'll text Geppetto: *"Going to NJ for the weekend. Enjoy the place to yourself."*

But my autocorrect *hates* NJ for some reason and replaces it with NO.

"*Going to NO for the weekend. ENOoy the place to yourself.*"

Now I know what iPhone really thinks of New Jersey.

Plus, my iPhone X even stops tracking my steps once we cross the Hudson River, and my stalkers are on standby until I take the 156 bus from Port Authority. After that, I'm untraceable, and therefore, killable.

## DECEMBER 12

*Dear Diary:*

I attended Carlos's work holiday party. It was an open bar and free food, which helped me realize I could grow six more arms like an octopus and have a drink in each. When there's free *anything*, I take without thinking. Carlos' blue balls are not because of lack of sex, but because I grab them so often I bruise them.

His balls are not the only thing I grab. When Carlos and I went on our road trip at the beginning of December, I stuffed my face with continental breakfast, stole a million stevia packets, and pocketed all the mini lotions at every motel.

Trust me, that's not enough. I take batteries out of remotes, toilet paper out of bathrooms, and clean tampons out of dead women.

Do you know what I've never touched, though? Donald Trump Jr.'s book: *Nothing Rhymes with Orange.*

## DECEMBER 13

*Dear Diary:*

Today is Friday the thirteenth, and while I should be scared, I'm not. Ever since I started drinking my cold brew through a reusable straw to save birds, I keep finding interesting facts about them.

I told my best friend Bagwis over the phone, "I wanna be like a bird!"

He said, "I see what you're saying, so you could be free and all that?"

I said, "No, fuck that. I'm a multitasker at heart, and I'd do just about anything to accomplish several tasks simultaneously."

"So what does it have to do with birds?"

"If I were a bird I could poop in free fall, which would save me an hour a day."

Bagwis hung up.


## DECEMBER 14

*Dear Diary:*

Yesterday two impeachment articles were passed to the House of Representatives, and Donald Trump may very well be the third sitting president who gets impeached! By the way, why do they say he's sitting? He's never sitting; he's always playing golf.

The Republicans run the Senate, so removing Trump from the White House will be as hard as removing Mama June from the refrigerator.

Also hard to remove:

1. A White Claw out of a white girl's hands.
2. A cum sting from my eye.
3. A hanger out of Julia Roberts's massive mouth.

## DECEMBER 15

*Dear Diary:*

My boss asked me to order two cases of this new brand of sparkling water called Ugly, so I did.

When the confirmation email came, the subject line read: *"Thanks for ordering Ugly."* Did they miss a comma? I forwarded the email to Susan Boyle.

I ordered the lemon-lime flavor, which would go great with my black beans and a margarita I'm planning to have for lunch—yes, I'm drinking at work, because fuck work. I love eating two to three cans of black beans (which makes me gassy), and then holiday-shopping in crowded stores where there are, suddenly, no lines!

I hate lines, and farting is the only way to get around them. When stores get *unbearably* crowded and I have no patience, I ask Winona Ryder to come along and shoplift with me.

## DECEMBER 16

*Dear Diary:*

I'm not sick but I called out anyway. My boss texted me: *"Feel better but don't overeat today. Since we have a presentation on Monday,* don't wear H&M pants and please, look under a hundred and forty pounds. Our clients don't wanna stare at a fat face."

He fat-shames *everyone*.

A girlfriend of mine hates her job the way I hate mine and calls out often, coming up with the most ridiculous excuses. Let's call her Halitosis Gabby (because that's her real name).

The last time she called out, Halitosis Gabby said, "I'm calling out because my iron is out of whack, which made my chastity belt rusty. When I went to the appointment with the colorectal surgeon and he needed access to my back door, we had to pry it open with a crowbar."

## DECEMBER 17

*Dear Diary:*

Today is my seven-month anniversary with Carlos, and he took me to a restaurant. Why is it that whenever people celebrate, they take their significant other to get fatter?

I'm gay (plus work for a company that's developing a *scale*), so I can't be overweight. I hope Carlos takes me to an activity that burns calories like a gym class, a bike ride, or a sex party. At the last one, we could get our exercise *and* protein. I'd do anything to lose weight, but I refuse to smoke tina to curb appetite.

My solution is to move to a developing country as, after all, North America is the land of plenty. I'm searching for a place without any food or judgment but with lots of action. I think I'll live in Ricky Martin's ass.

(PS. Carlos taught me how to say "tina" in Spanish. It's "Latina.")

## DECEMBER 18

*Dear Diary:*

President Trump is impeached!

Trump had it fucking coming to him. I don't even care that he won't be kicked out of office. It's the principle of the thing. You'll get punished when you do wrong. Have you never read *Crime and Punishment?*

I hate sexual predators like Harvey Weinstein or Jeffrey Epstein, but they either have no power or they're dead. Donald Trump, on the other hand, is our *president*. How did it happen that Trump became the most influential person in the world?

(Hint: the Russian hack.)

I'm not worried. Looking back, all giant predators got electrocuted (like James French) or got extinct (like dinosaurs or Taylor Lautner's career).

Trump's impeachment is a big win for the American people!

The news perked me up and I even started browsing for jobs (while still at work). I applied for position as an event planner, and if I don't get it I have nothing to lose (except for some holiday weight—according to my boss). He no longer makes me angry, and with less than two weeks left before 2020, that's the attitude I needed.

I feel careless, happy, and content.

## DECEMBER 19

*Dear Diary:*

I'm reading the news with my morning cup of cold brew and my morning wood. I'm already thirty minutes late for work, but I don't care anymore.

The following article caught my eye: "Woman beats man for the first time ever." I was so excited! Why did she beat him up? So I read on...

Turns out, the article is about a darts championship, and a woman beat a man.

What a disappointment! I'm tired of boring news. Brexit? Boring! Obesity? Double boring! Obesity is only fun when celebrities or one of my gay friends are concerned. And you know what's triple boring? Me, waiting for someone rich to die.

I have this recurring dream where I receive a phone call: My uncle died and left me three million dollars. I don't care about my uncle and if Judge Judy needs to see some tears, I'll pepper-spray my face. An article on CNN pops up: "Heartless Nephew Sprays Mace to Convince Judge He Loved His Uncle."

*That's* a good name for an article!

I don't know if it's a dream or a nightmare because when I wake up, nothing happens—nobody dies and my account isn't fatter by three million dollars.

As far as I'm aware, I have one uncle—singular—who lives in Siberia. Unless he's been saving for nine hundred years, we all know he doesn't have three liters of vodka, let alone three million dollars.

If you aren't born into wealth, if you don't steal, and if you're honest—don't expect to get rich. You'll get *comfortable*, but getting my face in Carlos's bush is also comfortable, and whose goal is to just be comfortable? Daddy wants to be rich!

## DECEMBER 20

*Dear Diary:*

Carlos took me to a show called *A Christmas Carol* on Broadway. Great show! It was all song and dance until the end of the show when it started snowing with fake snow made out of soap (or whatever they use on Broadway).

The woman behind me gasped loudly and said with a French accent, "I hope this soap is sulfate-free!"

I couldn't stop laughing. The Frenchy looked like her face needed a deep tissue massage from Jessica, not a sulfate-free soap. Besides, if you wish to avoid chemicals then don't bleach your hair, don't use lotion, and don't breathe—and she was doing all three. And yes, I said *breathe*; the air we breathe consists of chemicals: two parts hydrogen and one part oxygen, but for her it was one hundred parts stupid.

I get it, Frenchy: You want the best for your children. If you want the best for your children—and I'm speaking strictly from personal experience—then let them stay up past midnight, give them a generous allowance, and when the principal calls, stay on your child's side by saying, "Yes, Mr. Confuckus, you dumb fuckfuck. Honey Boo Boo wants to stay home today to catch up on her cartoons and to finish an entire pig roast, and if you have a problem with that, call the fucking police. Love, Mama June."

## DECEMBER 21

*Dear Diary:*

I've been so hard on Mama June lately, and it's almost Christmas, so I must be nice. Mama June, it's nothing personal.

I just hate June. The weather is hot and humid in June, and I can't afford baby powder for my sweaty ass.

I found a list of naughty names, which I stole from Santa's pants when I sat on his lap at Macy's. I don't care about the nice names, but if you wanna know, they were: Blah, Blah, and Blah.

The first three naughty ones, obviously starting from the most annoying, are: Anne Hathaway, Amy Adams, and Melania Trump (or Duck Lips as she's known).

I don't hate any of these people personally. Akin to Mama June, I simply hate their names. Besides, did you know how Duck Lips became famous? The brand Duck Commander built its empire working off of her duck calls.

Before marrying our newly-impeached president, Melania used to be Knavs. To change her name, she just crossed off Knavs and wrote Trump. The same amount of letters.

So fucking lazy!

## DECEMBER 22

*Dear Diary:*

I don't know what my roommate Geppetto eats, but somehow his excrements ricochet from the bowl and end up all over the toilet seat, and when Geppetto flushes the toilet the excrements float back up like the Unsinkable Molly Brown.

I'm trying to sell Geppetto to NASA on e-Bay. I heard NASA is developing an anti-sinking technology to assure that liners like the *R.M.S. Titanic* stay afloat. Onboard the ship they would serve all the food Geppetto eats, and when it's time to sink, the passengers would defecate all around and make it safely to New York.

Speaking of the number two, a third of our poop is dead bacteria and red blood cells. I read that on the internet so it must be true. But *how* can it be true? When you don't eat for a week, dead bacteria should still be coming out, right? But it doesn't. You don't eat, you don't shit. It's just good math.

## DECEMBER 23

*Dear Diary:*

I think the neck is useless. Even owls and the Olsen twins agree that necks are stupid, that's why they don't have them. What does the neck even do? It doesn't process alcohol, doesn't clean the blood, and doesn't fight infections. The neck occasionally lubricates the throat with mucus when you need to swallow something big, for instance, before a hotdog eating contest. Chris Christie practiced by swallowing whole tables. I heard that Chris Christie lost weight on the paleo diet. The Paleolithic diet means "to eat like your ancestors," so I'm not sure where Chris Christie finds dinosaur food.

Maybe I should give the paleo diet a try. Why not? First, though, I need to find the *shashka* sword because that's how my Russian ancestors hunted. I'd run naked around Astoria with the *shashka* sword and a hard-on, yelling, "I'm craving some Asian!!!"

## DECEMBER 24

*Dear Diary:*
Today is Christmas Eve. My beloved boyfriend took me to New Jersey to spend Christmas with his mom. I'm so happy and wanna wish Merry Christmas to everyone, especially those who don't have a family in the United States.
As we bypassed a football field full of soccer moms, I said, "Merry Christmas, mother soccers!"
Two guys sitting at a bus stop were sucking on some chicken wings, so I told them, "Merry Christmas, wing suckers!"
And then in the bedroom, I told Carlos, "Merry Christmas! Let's take some poppers!"


## DECEMBER 25

*Dear Diary:*
Happy birthday, Jesus!
I don't need any presents today because all I want for Christmas is to spend some quality time with my boyfriend...
... said no one ever! I'm greedy when it comes to presents. The more, the merrier!
Note to self: Remind Carlos I would like a sweater in size extra small and a diamond ring from Tiffany's in size nine and a half.
I've been coaching Carlos about my sizes (shoes, fingers, and underwear) but it's tricky. For a sweater, for example, I'm an M, but in my lucid dreams I'm an S, and if Carlos gets me anything larger than XS I'll punch him so hard that he'll need to call SOS.

Diary, I'm so rude! It's just when presents and Tiffany's are concerned, I get fucking violent!

## DECEMBER 26

*Dear Diary:*
　I'm having an onset of bad diarrhea. My ass is attacking the toilet bowl. Pow-pow, pew-pew. Two more minutes of this, and I'm calling the cops on myself.
　My dung is all over the toilet seat, all over the fuzzy pink lid, and even on the ceiling.
　Never mind! I tried to scrape it from the ceiling but it's dry, so it must be from the last time.
　I mean, why is my ass shooting? Is it a gun? If that's a yes, then here's an ad for it:
　"This ass is a dangerous weapon with an extra-wide, 0.38 caliber.[1] The ass is semi-automatic, twelve-round extended grip, and it has a clean, crisp trigger. This award-winning ass was featured on QVC as the product of the year. It's lightweight, easy to conceal, and rated +P."
　So what I'm saying is, my ass should be sold at a gun shop. Don't judge me, I just need some extra pocket money.

[1] I looked it up and "caliber" basically means "hole." So I guess in gun lingo my caliber is tight.

## DECEMBER 27

*Dear Diary:*

Bagwis—who is also broke—told me, "This season, I don't need any *presents* from you. All I care about is your *presence*."

I said, "That may be true for you but it's not for me. Don't passive-aggressively tell me that you won't be sending me any presents this season."

"Not passive-aggressively, I just told you that I won't be getting any."

I said, "Well, bitch, I'll send you my 'presence'! I'll call ICE on you—the Institute of Culinary Education. They will chop you up and I'll sell your kidneys on the black market. Either way, I'm getting a present this season, and it's so sweet of you!"

## DECEMBER 28

*Dear Diary:*

The year is coming to an end, and I realized that while I didn't learn much Spanish, I can say basic things. Let's envision I walked into a gay bar in Guadalajara, which I think is somewhere in Mexico. I can walk up to a gaggle of gay men and say, "Hola, chicos. Got some leche?"

I can now correctly pronounce Ariana Grande, Jennifer Lopez, and Sofia Vergara without an accent. Most importantly, I learned that "woman" is *mujer*, "man" is *hombre*, and "gay man" is HOMOmbre.

**DECEMBER 29**

*Dear Diary:*

The hair on my head looks incredibly thick and healthy, meaning finasteride works! (At least one of us wants to work.) I remember how twelve months ago my hair was so limp I had to buy it a wheelchair. My pubic bush has also doubled in size and I no longer care that it makes me weigh fifty pounds heavier! It's so big that when I fell yesterday while drunk, the bush acted like a cushion and I bounced right up!

**DECEMBER 30**

*Dear Diary:*

Today is New Year's Eve's eve, and I bought my drag queen friend Steve a new weave, I bought Geppetto a small candle for his BDSM fantasies (he likes dripping wax on his nipples), I bought Anna from Louisiana what she needs the most (a book of manners, *Plumbers' Guide to Toilets*), I bought Bagwis a douche so we could both save bees, and lastly, I bought new banana-flavored, low-carb, low-sugar edible panties for Carlos.

Daddy's feeling generous this holiday season! Or, rather, the American Express is feeling generous.

It feels as if just yesterday I woke up and it was still January. I was complaining about being fat, broke, and single. Today, I'm slightly overweight, I have *some* savings, and I have a boyfriend. And I saved a million animals—was it rhinos or turtles?—by drinking through reusable straws, and I feel better about myself for helping the environment! And don't forget how many bees I saved by douching and fertilizing the soil.

Back in January, I hated my demanding boss and my Harvard-educated, privileged coworkers. I hated that I was the only immigrant at the office who didn't deserve a raise, while everyone else talked about buying apartments and spending summers in the Hamptons. To sum up how I feel about that office, I'll quote a French singer Mylene Farmer: "Fuck them all." I know I've been hard on the French but it's only because I'm jealous of the French paradox where they eat all they want but stay skinny and healthy. So, while we're at it, fuck the French too.

I hated the product the company I was working for has developed, "the visual scale," which keeps telling you how fat you are by just looking at you. Trust me when I say this: nobody wants that. Right, Mama June?

So I finally quit my job!

Yes, I did! However, my boss doesn't know about it yet, so don't tell him. I plan to stop showing up until I get fired. And after *that*, I'll quit, right after depositing my first unemployment check.

## DECEMBER 31

*Dear Diary:*

I can't believe today is the last day of 2019. I'm feeling bittersweet. I've accomplished so much this year and I'm unsure whether I can top myself next year. The only way I could top something is by literally topping Carlos, but that will never happen—I'm a gold star gay and a gold star bottom.

I got a new job as an event organizer, so I sent an email to my boss with, *"Chupame, puta—that's Spanish for goodbye."* You get what you pay for, and he thought what, that because I'm an uneducated immigrant he can treat me like I deserve nothing? I know what I'm worth now, so he deserves what he pays for, which is nothing.

Fear made me stay for way too long, but courage rescued me.

I'm starting my new job in two weeks, so I must pre-suck Carlos in advance as I'll be busy for the next few months.

Most importantly, I have a boyfriend now, which is precisely what I wished for in January. He loves me for *me*, not because I'm rich, young, or skinny. I'm none of those things!

My hair is thicker, my face is thinner, and my ass is juicier after running on a treadmill every day.

At the beginning of the year, I assumed I was jealous and bitter because of my job, debt, or body issues. Turns out, I was resentful because I hated myself, and hating yourself is the worst. We are our worst judges.

I sound so fucking grownup, like Oprah, or at least like Bagwis. He went to high school.

Anyhow, Diary. I must run for my party, and since Carlos gave me another diary for Christmas as a present, I'll be back writing tomorrow. Happy New Year!

Or, if you're German: *guten* tuck.

If you're Celiac: *gluten* tuck.

And, if you're a drag queen: *happy* tuck.

# THE END

# FINAL NOTE

I do not personally hate any people I mention in this diary, especially those who I have invented as a joke. I do not believe all gay men pop drugs for lunch, much like I do not believe Mama June has a fence in her mouth. (I think she has tile from her bathroom.) Stereotypes are persistent, which is why I bring up everything—fat-shaming, homophobia, and ageism—because we need to fight that. If you still feel like I have offended you personally somehow and you have a strong need to vent, feel free to send hate mail to Homochitto National Forest in Mississippi. But if you want to save a Forever Stamp and your dignity, simply recycle your letter in a designated recycling area instead.

# ACKNOWLEDGMENTS

Thanks to my editors, Carlos and Jess, who made sure I do not sound like a complete moron. Now I only sound like half a moron. A very special thanks to Michael McMurtrey for getting involved and the entire cover design team.

Thanks, Dan Avery and Jeff Stotsky, for clarifying a few grammar (or as I call them New York) things. Only New Yorkers will say, "I live *on* the Upper East Side." Or "Are you *on* line?"

Yes, I'm *on*line! Shopping *on* fucking Amazon.

Thanks Nikita for believing in me!

Also, in no particular order (starting from whom I hate the most), thank you, Gian, Chance, and Jonathan. Your opinions do not matter! Just kidding. You do not have any opinions. Just kidding again. I am not thanking you. But I do miss you, assholes. Or as we say in Spanish, assjoles.

# ABOUT THE AUTHOR

Jeremy Taylor performed his first standup on a bus in Kazakhstan at the age of nine, which he writes about in his memoir. Since then, he wrote and performed comedy spasmodically.

In college, he scripted and starred in *KVN*,[1] an abbreviation for "the club of funny and witty people," which consists of standup, musical, sketch, and improv elements—and is a national competition akin to NBC's *Last Comic Standing*.

After immigrating to the United States from Russia, Jeremy performed standup in New York City.

Books that make him laugh are *I Hate Everyone Starting with Me* by Joan Rivers, *My Horizontal Life: A Collection of One-Night Stands* by Chelsea Handler, *Are You There God? It's Me, Margaret* by Judy Blume, and *R Is for Ricochet* by Sue Grafton.

His favorite TV shows are *I Love Lucy*, *Crazy Ex-Girlfriend*, *Kim's Convenience*, *Schitt's Creek*, *Friends*, *Sex and the City*, *Broad City*, *Emily in Paris*, *It's Always Sunny in Philadelphia*, *The Good Place*, *Saturday Night Life*, *Young & Hungry*, *Never Have I Ever*, and *Moesha*.

Books by Jeremy Taylor: *Smart Casual: And Other Expressions I Hate*; a novel, *The Cornerstones of Happiness*; and a memoir, *Noodles with Grandma: And Other Stories from Our Homestead in Kazakhstan*.

Instagram: jeremy.taylor.ny
Twitter: jeremytaylor_ny

---

[1] "KVN . . . is a Soviet and then Russian humour [sic] TV show and an international competition where teams (usually college students) compete by giving funny answers to questions and showing prepared sketches, that originated in the Soviet Union. . . ." Source: Wikipedia

www.ingramcontent.com/pod-product-compliance
Lightning Source LLC
Chambersburg PA
CBHW021822090426
42811CB00032B/1979/J